Praise for Rhonda Sciortino and *Successful Survivors*

"*Successful Survivors* helps survivors of trauma by showing them that it is possible to recover and to thrive following trauma—a message from which we can all benefit."
—Dr. Karen Bergstrom, Executive Director, Safe Families

"*Successful Survivors* tells what we foster parents have known all along, that people who have experienced severe adversity can become some of the strongest, most resilient and resourceful people around. Many survivors of abuse have used the character traits within them to create successful lives, and this book will help many more to do the same."
—Irene Clements, Executive Director,
National Foster Parent Association

"It is my wish for every person who had a rough childhood to let their painful experiences develop in them the characteristics described in this book. If they do that, and if they are honest and hard-working, they can create a good life for themselves."
—Tom Monaghan, founder of Domino's Pizza and Chancellor,
Ave Maria University

"Each of us has a cause for which we were created. Along with that cause we have the seeds of the characteristics we'll need to fulfill our unique cause. *Successful Survivors* gives practical advice for nurturing, developing, and leveraging those characteristics necessary for success."
—Matthew Barnett, founder of The Dream Center and
New York Times bestselling author, *The Cause within You*

"Rhonda captures your heart with her powerful story of surviving against all odds. She has the reader dig deep to mine the nuggets of truth that chases away the darkness and lights your world! No matter how bleak the day, no matter where you are in your journey, you can rise above your circumstances. Powerful...motivating...a must read!"
—Wayne Tesch, Co-Founder, Royal Family KIDS

"*Successful Survivors* shows us that we have within us the seeds of greatness that, when nurtured, are the characteristics we can use to fulfill our unique purpose."
—Mark Tennant, Founder, ALL IN Family Ministries and
Arrow Child & Family Ministries

"Rhonda's message of not being too broken to be fixed comes through loud and clear in *Successful Survivors*. Every one of us can mine the lessons out of the adversity we've experienced and use those lessons to create our own unique brand of successful living."

—Sandie Morgan, Ph.D., R.N., Director of Vanguard University's
Global Center for Women and Justice

"Experience as a psychologist and foster parent has shown me that resilience, persistence, determination, and all the other character traits of successful survivors truly do overcome adversity. Not only does *Successful Survivors* tell of these important traits and how to develop them, but it illustrates the point through true-life examples of successful survivors of adversity."

—Dr. John DeGarmo, leading foster care and parenting expert

"Trauma can make people feel isolated, and when trauma involves personal violence, it often leads to feelings of being unwanted and unloved. So the logical solution to the sense of isolation and being unwanted is to be included by people who identify and celebrate the value within. *Successful Survivors* does exactly that. It shows us through the stories of successful survivors that we have valuable character traits that can connect us to others and be the catalyst for healing broken hearts."

—Amelia Franck Meyer, M.S., M.S.W., A.P.S.W., L.I.S.W.,
CEO, Alia (www.aliainnovations.org)

"*Successful Survivors* embodies the hopeful voice that resonates throughout Rhonda's courageous life story of overcoming difficult odds. The power of this book is its ability to identify characteristics of greatness that will encourage and equip a generation of survivors to reach their fullest, God-given potential."

—Mark Rodgers, Principal, The Clapham Group

"Too many people live lives of quiet desperation, believing that there is no hope for success for them. Yet, within each of us are the gifts we need to succeed in living with meaning and purpose. *Successful Survivors* blasts the myth that there is no hope, and shows readers how they can turn the adversity they've experienced into their greatest advantage and share their strengths with others!"

—Derenda Schubert, Ph.D., Licensed Psychologist,
Bridge Meadows Executive Director

"*Successful Survivors* shifts our focus from the superficial to the substantive—the characteristics that can be honed to create and enjoy a good life."

—Marty Dutch, Assistant Vice President, Philanthropy Services,
First Foundation

"The stories of people who have used the character traits within them to create successful lives following serious adversity inspires us all to dig deep, identify our untapped potential, and to succeed, not just despite what we've been through, but specifically because of having been forced to use those character traits that were in us all along."

  —Kim Phagan-Hansel, editor of *Fostering Families Today* and
  The Kinship Parenting Toolbox

"*Successful Survivors* overflows with hope! Everyone who's gone through some kind of trauma would benefit from reading this book."

  —Connie R. Clendenan, M.S.W., CEO Valley Teen Ranch

"*Successful Survivors* says what Royal Family KIDS stands for—the truth that each of us has untapped potential within us. There is value in each of us, and *Successful Survivors* helps us find it in ourselves and others."

  —Christian Carmichael, President, Royal Family KIDS

"Young people who have faced adversity are capable of doing amazing things in life. A key component to reaching that level of success is the list of character traits Rhonda breaks down in *Successful Survivors*. This is a message that needs to be told in a big way!"

  —Jordan Bartlett, Director of Good, Doing Good Works

"Though hundreds of books have been written by people who come from brokenness, how many of those stories include life lessons to help us reframe the past? How many offer tools to keep us in moving forward? Rhonda is a person I trust to give us direction on how to flip our story to work for us, instead of against us!"

  —Glenn Garvin, author, *A Seed of Hope in Toxic Soil*

"Rhonda shares her passion and insight born from personal experience about how trials, struggles, and hardships—no matter how bad they were—can forge in us great gifts. These gifts are traits that can be used to walk a pathway to a successful life instead of living a life of defeat and victimhood. She does not say the experiences were good, but what they can end up creating in us are golden. Rhonda is a force of nature, much of whose genesis was born out of horrific circumstances that she has used to help achieve great things."

  —Ron L. Storm, M.S., Moody Global Ministries

"Every one of us can operate at genius level, and *Successful Survivors* connects the dots between the trauma we experience and our personal genius that leads to success."

  —Scott Henderson, Head Dot Connector, Doing Good Works

"Life change happens when our thinking is transformed, and that is the power of *Successful Survivors*. Rhonda champions people to turn their pain into purpose and live an abundantly successful life."
　　　　　—Crystal Van Kempen-McClanahan, Ed.D.

"Rhonda's writing is pure and powerful. Her book inspires and encourages us all to embrace our tough beginnings, turn our pain into progress, and then watch our disappointments transform into our destiny. This is a must read for everyone that's ever heard those crushing words: "You can't"...because Rhonda Sciortino proves that YOU CAN!"
　　　　　—Brian D. Molitor, Founder, Molitor International

"Rhonda Sciortino is a force to be reckoned with. Her ability to communicate the ins and outs of how to be a successful survivor stems from her experience with some of the toughest circumstances anyone could live through. Not only has she gone from survival to success, but she's showing others how to run after their destiny and to be a successful survivor too."
　　　　　—Torrian Scott, author of *Running After Destiny*
　　　　　and Founder, Masters in the Marketplace

"Two words appear often in *Successful Survivors*: 'value' and 'hope'. It is well established in business that all sales situations degenerate to price in the absence of a value interpreter. So it is with people. If they can't see their value, they rarely don't have hope. But just inspiring hope isn't enough if it can't be sustained—for that, they need to see a pathway out. *Successful Survivors* provides that pathway as only Rhonda Sciortino can."
　　　　　—Robert J. Martin, Vice-Chair, Alliance for HOPE International

"I know far too many people who think they are trapped by their childhood experiences. Rhonda's message in *Successful Survivors* is perfect for helping them break out of that trap and find success. I cannot wait to give copies of this book to family, friends, and clients."
　　　　　—Deborah Ausburn, former foster parent
　　　　　and attorney for youth organizations

Successful Survivors

The 8 Character Traits
of Survivors

and How You Can

Attain Them

Rhonda Sciortino

hatherleigh
Improve your life. Change your world.

Successful Survivors
Text copyright © 2016 Rhonda Sciortino

Library of Congress Cataloging-in-Publication Data
is available upon request.
ISBN: 978-1-57826-629-6

Interior Design by Cynthia Dunne

Printed in the United States
10 9 8 7 6 5 4 3 2 1

Contents

Contents

This book is dedicated to Anna Sciortino
and all the other successful survivors
who leave their sorrows at the door,
put a smile on their faces,
and go to work
in spite of what they've been through.
Their perseverance and determination are an inspiration to others.

And with gratitude
to Nick, who teaches loyalty with his life;
to Sarah, who refuses to give up on anyone;
and to Enrique, whose adaptability and
calm temperament steadies us all.

Acknowledgments

I AM A SUCCESSFUL survivor of abandonment, childhood abuse, poverty, homelessness, and hunger. I now have a wonderful family, healthy relationships with genuine friends, a satisfying career, peace, joy, good health, and financial stability. I attribute the success attained in every area of my life to relationships, albeit sometimes brief, with people who recognized in me some of the characteristics we'll be discussing within these pages. For me, these people include a foster father I was with for a very short time, two elementary school teachers, my high school typing teacher, the insurance agent who gave me my first job when I was 15, an elderly insurance broker who took me under his wing and taught me what he had learned when he started selling insurance door to door after WWII, and the [then] CEO of Hillview Acres Children's Home, H.H. "Corky" Kindsvater, MSW. Of course there have been others along the way for whom I am forever grateful, but it was these people whom I've mentioned here, who saw something good in me long before I saw anything good in myself, who led me to dare to believe that there was a good purpose for my life and that there just might be some hope of a good future for me.

Foreword

WE ARE ALL searching for hope, meaning, and purpose in our lives. The good news is that we each already hold the key to our life's cause—it's the unique cause and calling that was placed in our hearts.

I found my cause when I found myself at the intersection of the needs of others and what I was able to do. I let go of my dreams of building what I thought was a big, "successful" church and began following God's dream for my life. It turns out that instead of building a church, I was called to help build people. That's what we do at The Dream Center in Los Angeles, and at all the other independent Dream Centers throughout the country. What "success" looks like for me is very different from what I anticipated. Instead of serving a congregation of a few thousand people, the Dream Center (often referred to as "the church that never sleeps") serves more than 30,000 people *every week*!

Rhonda Sciortino found her unique cause at the intersection of the needs of child welfare organizations and her expertise in insurance. When she took her first job in insurance at age 15, little did she know that the true cause placed in her heart would be to help people who have been mistreated to find and fulfill the unique purpose for their lives—and to do it by way of protecting people and organizations that care for kids and families.

Everyone's cause and calling is different, and the paths we take to get there are as diverse as you can imagine. But the common thread for all of us is that finding and fulfilling our purpose requires strength, persistence, determination, courage, and the other characteristics of successful survivors.

Lots of people judge their characteristics by their past, believing they're not optimistic, able to adapt, or courageous. But Rhonda shows

us that even if we were not born with a strong measure of these characteristics, it doesn't matter! We can hone the ones we have and develop
a measure of the ones we don't, and ultimately do what we were born
to do.

—Matthew Barnett, founder of The Dream Center
and *New York Times* bestselling author,
The Cause within You

Introduction

You Have Assets You Haven't Yet Leveraged

WE ALL WANT to be accepted—both by ourselves and by others. Many of us spend our entire lives striving to be good enough; yet even at our peaks, we find ourselves falling just short of this illusory goal.

The purpose of this book is to help you see that you are not only good enough, but that in fact, you are perfectly equipped to do exactly what you were created to do, and be what you were born to be. In other words, you already have everything you need to be your best self—you just don't know it yet.

There may even be things about you that you see as flaws; there may be events in your past that you think have made you unworthy or unlovable. Believe it or not, these are the very things that make you qualified to fulfill your purpose—to be who you were meant to be.

Every one of us has a story; everyone has felt pain (some of us more so than others). But there is no point in comparing adversities and obstacles; to the one who is suffering, the pain is not viewed objectively, not considered in variety or degree—it is simply *real*. And while some people come through adversity stronger than before, others seem to suffer endlessly in a perpetual cycle.

The important thing for all survivors of traumatic experiences to realize is that it is *their choice* whether to mine the lessons from their pain and move past it, or else be poisoned by it. Every moment that we think about the hurt we've endured or the person or situation that caused the pain, we commit a voluntary, *unnecessary* error—we give up another moment of our lives to that pain. Haven't we, as survivors, spent enough time on the painful events in our lives? Why relive them again and again, thinking about them, talking about them—with friends, co-workers, counselors, and anyone else who will listen? You deserve better. Rather than dwelling on the past, and talking about what happened or who was involved, it's time for a change. It's time to find what good can come from past pains by leverage what we've learned to become *successful survivors*.

Many people think that no good comes from painful experiences. Some would even say that I'm insensitive for even suggesting such a notion. But believe me when I say that I know what I'm talking about when it comes to surviving pain. Abandoned by my parents and raised by my mentally ill grandfather and my drug-addicted, alcoholic grandmother, I was brought up in a filthy shack the size of a small garage. For most of the first 16 years of my life, I lived in poverty and hunger. I was beaten, burned, yelled at, and cursed out for every reason under the sun (or for no reason at all). I emancipated myself from my status as a ward of the court in California's child welfare system at age 16. I worked hard, saved my money, and bought my first house at 19, and I purchased my first rental property at 22. I started my first business at 27, and ultimately established, built, and sold two successful companies. I did all of this while my childhood neighbors went on to use and sell drugs, join gangs, have teenage pregnancies, and receive government assistance for years. Now, I write books and speak all over the United States, doing media appearances and radio shows, all to help others succeed—not just in spite of, but specifically *because* of what they have been through.

What's the difference between them and me? It's not that I was smarter, prettier, luckier, or more talented. The difference is two-fold: first, I realized that the skills I developed and the abilities I needed to succeed in business all came from everything I had *already* survived. That revelation helped me to quit feeling sorry for myself and move beyond feeling that the world, and everyone in it, owed me something. Once I was secure in the belief that there *was* something good about me, and that I *did* have the potential to succeed, my determination to unlock my potential began to develop. The second, and most important difference between my success and the failure of my childhood peers, was my faith. I truly believe that the success I now enjoy in every area of my life is the exponential reward for the combination of my willingness to do the work necessary to find and fulfill the good plan for my life, multiplied by the power of God. But regardless of your personal faith, or even lack thereof, I encourage you to believe that there is something good about you; that there is a purpose for your life, and that you can find and fulfill it.

The concept that we are who we are specifically *because* of the pain we have endured is a difficult one for many people to accept. But the truth is that we all are who we are because of the events that influenced our lives and molded our character, regardless of whether those influences and their results are good or bad. Accepting this truth doesn't condone what happened, but what's done is done—you can't go back and change your past. But you *can* turn negative events in your past into something positive, by mining the lessons out of your experiences and leveraging the character strengths and coping mechanisms you've developed through that pain.

Whenever you feel yourself tempted to dwell on the trauma you've experienced or the people who hurt you, I challenge you to deliberately consider one of your positive personality traits. For example, when I consider that my mother and father left me with the very people who had so abused my mother, it's easy to feel anger toward them, and pity for myself. But I've come to recognize that those negative emotions lead to a completely unproductive state of mind. Instead, I consider the fact that, as a result of the abandonment and loneliness of my childhood, I learned to be independent and self-reliant, and to be content with being alone. As the CEO of my own company, I found that independence and self-reliance served me well; as such, the experiences that resulted in those characteristics didn't bother me as they might have others.

As a result of poverty, I learned to be resourceful. I learned how to get by on next to nothing, and how to fix things that were broken because I couldn't afford to buy a replacement. This resourcefulness has served me well in many areas of life. For example, it was this resourcefulness that led me to figure out what I called "work-arounds" when it seemed there was no way to accomplish what needed to be done on the limited budget of a young entrepreneur with no resources, no family, and no safety net.

As a result of the abuse I suffered, I was bold enough to take risks, including leaving a good job to go into business for myself. I figured that a business failure couldn't hurt as much as those childhood beatings had. The pain of my childhood also made me strong enough to deal with the inevitable setbacks in business, ones that would have devastated other people. I also gained the empathy and the burning desire to see justice done for abuse victims that cannot be learned from a textbook in a classroom. These qualities empowered me to protect people and organizations that care for abused children, which has been my life's work for over 30 years. The physical and emotional abuse I endured when I was too little to protect myself "inoculated" me, serving as a vaccine for the inevitable challenges and adversities I would face in the business world.

But this mining or digging up of lessons and characteristics from adversity isn't unique to me or my life. Every one of us has acquired characteristics that can help us succeed, both personally and professionally. We can mine these characteristics, coping mechanisms and lessons from all of our experiences—even from the most painful of them. The "good news" is, the more traumatic the experience, the more significant the lessons we can learn, and the stronger our successful survivor characteristics can become. But before we can accomplish this important, transformational work, we must first change the view we have of ourselves.

Survivors of adversity must change their mindset from being a victim to being a survivor. The truth is, victims are often repeatedly victimized; survivors survive. Once we've made the powerful shift in our thinking from victim to survivor, the next step is to rise up to the next level, becoming a "successful survivor." Successful survivors don't just survive—they *thrive*. They grow stronger after overcoming adversity. And the pivotal step to this important progression is nothing more than one's choice of mindset and attitude.

Successful survivors are strong, capable, resilient, tenacious, courageous, resourceful, and so much more—characteristics that are valuable in every relationship, every industry, and every profession. While each successful survivor may not have every one of the characteristics included here, each of them has at least one that has been instrumental in helping them through difficult times. All these characteristics can be acquired, developed, and leveraged to unlock and unleash the potential trapped inside those who have survived trauma. Perhaps surprisingly, many successful survivors go on to express gratitude for having experienced the painful events of their lives! Many people say that, had they not experienced the pain, they wouldn't have become who they are.

There is an enormous difference between being a *survivor* and being a *successful survivor*. A liar, a cheat, or a murderer may be a *survivor* of child abuse or some other traumatic experience, but his or her behavior would suggest that he or she is anything *but* successful. On the other hand, a person with a good job, a great family, and a terrific attitude may have experienced similar abuse or trauma, but based on his or her daily life, you would never know about his or her past. Both examples are of survivors—but only one is a *successful* survivor.

Why do some people who experience abandonment, abuse, neglect, serious illness or injury, loss of a loved one, or some other trauma triumph over tragedy, while others go on to live marginal, desperate, or even criminal lives? More importantly, how can we intervene and help these people to overcome hardship before irreparable damage is done? Although the process can become quite complicated, the root of healing and growth is simple. In fact, the answer can be summarized in one word: *relationships*.

The people we choose to share our lives with have an incredible impact not only on the path our lives take, but the way we see ourselves.

Other people have the ability to see us in an objective sort of way that we cannot ourselves perceive. But the people who influence us the most profoundly, those who serve as catalysts to our transformation, do not have to be those closest to us. In some cases, it's a random person who makes an observation we've never heard before that opens our eyes to the goodness in us. A bank teller or grocery clerk can pay us a compliment that opens our eyes to a personality trait or characteristic that we may have never previously considered.

I've spoken to many mental health professionals while seeking answers to the question of why some trauma victims do so poorly in life, while others go on to do so well. I've interviewed countless adult victims of childhood abuse, as well as successful survivors of other types of traumatic experiences, including survivors of imprisonment during WWII, victims of human trafficking, those involved in life-threatening automobile accidents, and much more. You'll have a chance to hear some of their compelling stories later on. I've heard stories of heart-warming outcomes and stories of heart-wrenching results; and in doing so, I've come to some conclusions. In every case where a survivor of trauma has achieved a fruitful life, there is at least one person who took an interest in the person, who took the time to find something good about the survivor, to point it out and in so doing let the person know that he or she is valuable. That feeling of being liked and valued can be the beginning of a relationship, one that can change the trajectory of the lives of both people.

Al Siebert, Ph.D., spent more than 40 years studying the phenomenon of survival. He gained valuable insights into the qualities and habits that help people overcome difficult situations, from everyday conflicts to potentially overwhelming life stresses. Dr. Siebert founded the Al Siebert Resiliency Center in Portland, Oregon. He also authored *The Survivor Personality, The Resiliency Advantage,* and numerous articles wherein he asserted that the characteristics of survivors aren't found solely in people who were born with them; rather, they can be developed. This is

a hugely important point. Dr. Siebert emphasizes that altho
vidual may not have a natural bent toward survival skills, lik
or self-reliance, it does not mean the individual cannot develo

Dr. Lawrence Calhoun and Dr. Richard Tedeschi, professors at the University of North Carolina at Charlotte and co-authors of *Trauma and Transformation: Growing in the Aftermath of Suffering* and *Posttraumatic Growth: Positive Changes in the Aftermath of Crisis*, have spent a lifetime researching post-traumatic stress growth. That's *growth*, not *disorder*, and their research shows that, although it is not guaranteed, it is certainly possible to become stronger after trauma or crisis.

Barbara Fredrickson, Ph.D., author of the book, *Positivity*, has researched the influence of positive thinking over the circumstances of one's life. Dr. Fredrickson's research has revealed new strategies for bouncing back from set-backs, for connecting with others, and for new possibilities available for becoming the best versions of ourselves.

The work of these and other researchers and professors in what is now commonly referred to as "the positive psychology movement" shows that people can not only *survive* trauma—they can learn to *thrive* from it. Within the books of these and other researchers, we see over and over again that **trauma is not necessarily a predictor of a life sentence of adversity**.

It is true that these characteristics can come more naturally to some than to others. But it is also true that anyone who is willing to do the work can develop a level of proficiency in each of these key survival skills. Consider a musician born with natural talent. Though she may be less skilled than a child prodigy, she can still be trained to become a proficient musician, capable of creating beautiful and worthwhile music. In the same way, all of the characteristics of successful survivors can be developed to some degree. We are each born with a seed of these characteristics in us. These seeds do not grow in the good times; rather, they develop and mature in the hard times.

My hope with this book is two-fold, the first of which is to help people who have experienced trauma to recognize their strengths within these pages. When we identify good things about ourselves, we feel better. When we feel better, we make better choices. Making better choices leads to better results, and ultimately to becoming a successful survivor. The second part of my hope for this book is that it will spark a shift in our culture, that we might begin to value these enduring, defining characteristics more than we do material things, celebrity gossip, and fame-for-fame's-sake. If, as a culture, we can learn to recognize and celebrate these qualities that together make up the best of humanity, my hope is that we could motivate people to move away from living as a "victim," toward a desire to develop the characteristics of successful survivors—and to subsequently enjoy the good life that follows.

No matter what has happened to you, or what you've done or failed to do, you can mine lessons from the adversity you've experienced to release the potential trapped inside you. Doing this work can be transformational—and you are the only one who can do it.

Whether you're someone who has been through some unfair experiences, or if you care about someone who has been hurt, keep reading. Find the characteristics that can be acquired and developed to meaningfully and measurably change your life and the lives of those within your influence. Don't just survive—become a *successful survivor.*

CHAPTER 1

Strength and Determination

STRONG: especially able, competent, or powerful
DETERMINED: resolved, resolute, or unwavering

L OUIE ZAMPARINI SURVIVED being shot down in his fighter jet during WWII, being lost in the shark-infested Pacific Ocean without food or water for 47 days, and endured two years of torture in a Japanese prisoner of war camp. Because Louie was known by his captors as having been an Olympic athlete, he was saved from execution, but he was also singled out for particularly vicious tortures. In the years after his release, he converted to Christianity, forgave his captors, published his autobiography, *Devil at My Heels*, and became an inspirational speaker. In his 90s, Mr. Zamparini was still speaking in churches, telling his story and encouraging others. He was known to say, "When you go through horrific experiences, you become more hardy."

Survivors of severe trauma are often stronger than the average person. When adversity strikes, some people are overwhelmed, while others take the crisis more or less in stride, despite their own feelings of terror, sadness, or anger.

Successful survivors seem to be able to put their painful current events into proper perspective. They've lived through difficult situations before, so they intuitively know that their present challenges are temporary. For every successfully navigated challenge, they gain perspective in regards to their options, which helps them to continue moving forward, despite the circumstances and the powerful emotions that may be involved. This perspective allows them to navigate through the stages involved in dealing with their current circumstances, while processing their feelings so that they ultimately arrive at a place of strength. Every successfully navigated challenge builds their confidence and allows them to take calculated risks, moving forward boldly, secure in the knowledge that they can make it through anything.

Perhaps Mr. Zamparini's survival can be attributed to the strong-willed defiance he exhibited as a child, as recounted in Laura Hillenbrand's best-selling book, *Unbroken: A World War II Story of Survival, Resilience, and Redemption.* Or perhaps it is his track and field training to be an Olympic athlete that prepared him to persevere through the hardships he experienced during WWII. Or perhaps it is a combination of these things, along with an individual strength, tenacity, and determination to survive that were "hard wired" into Louis Zamparini, all of which worked together to help him survive.

Sadly, some of those who face adversity become mired in their anger, denial, or their feeling that life has been unfair to them, effectively halting any forward progress in their lives. We've all known people who spend their lives believing that they've been dealt a bad hand by fate. They don't try new things, fearing an increase in what they perceive as unfairness or some other additional harm.

Strength is a powerful characteristic found within every successful survivor to some degree, borne of the pain they've experienced. Because of past adversity, they have learned how to process pain and grieve losses better than those who haven't had the opportunity to go through tough times. Having been forced to dig deep and tap into whatever it takes to get through, successful survivors are better equipped to process, or even *embrace* future conflict. It's not that successful survivors haven't experienced unfairness; some of them have been victims of violent crime or other extremely unfair circumstances. This strength is part of the difference between survivors and those who are *successful survivors*—it is the foundation of their broader perspective. They are able to tell themselves that whatever they're going through is *not* "the end of the world." They give themselves permission to grieve the loss for a time, and then they close the chapter on the painful event, put it in its proper place, and move on.

You may know people who have lost their jobs and spiraled down into extended depression; while others, dealing with similar circumstances, instead regroup, put together a new resume or business plan, and get to work doing whatever they can to move them forward into a future that they trust will be as good or better than what they've lost. Some people take the adversity of a lost job to another level, seeing it as a challenge and an opportunity to step back and reassess their lives. Rather than make themselves sick and irritable, lying awake at night and wondering what's going to happen, how they'll pay their bills, and how they'll provide for their families, they see the "time off" as a respite from the rat race that traps so many people. Exceptionally strong people actually get *excited* about the opportunity to strategically and deliberately plan the next chapter of their lives.

Successful survivors view the loss of a job (or any other loss, for that matter) as their opportunity to "hit the reset button" on their lives. They may go back to school to learn something entirely new, create a business plan and launch out into a new business venture, or find a new job with new opportunities, which afford them the ability to explore an industry they may never have otherwise considered. You can see where people with this mindset might even see themselves in a more favorable position than others who feel trapped in jobs they barely tolerate, fearful of making a career change because of their reliance on the income from that job, knowing that a change to a different job or industry will likely result in reduced income, which won't pay the bills they've acquired. And so they remain trapped, while the successful survivor surveys a world full of brand new opportunities.

But for some, the challenge they face is that of an irreparable tragedy, such as the death of a loved one. Even in cases where no amount of effort or good attitude can change one's circumstances, there is still a choice to be made: the choice to "put on" a good attitude is ours alone to make. **No one can force you to suffer if you choose not to suffer.** If this sounds absurd, consider Viktor Frankl's powerful message in his book *Man's Search for Meaning*. His story of surviving Nazi death camps and maintaining hope has been life-altering for countless people. If Frankl could choose to remain hopeful and use his imagination to envision a brighter future, even under those unimaginable circumstances, *you* can do it with all the advances and advantages of the 21st century.

Strong people see adversity as an opportunity to improve their lives. They *choose* to see adversity as the channel through which their dreams can emerge. This *doesn't* mean they don't feel anger or sadness about what's happened, or about the unfairness they've experienced. It means that they don't allow the anger to become bitterness, or the sadness to become depression. It means that they make a deliberate effort to shift from those unproductive feelings of grief and loss to a sense of hope for the future, regardless of how dim the light of that future may be, and how real and painful the unfair events are. Some people harness their anger into the determination to seek success, the sweetest revenge of all. Others, like Viktor Frankl, use their sadness to turn their tragedy into something meaningful. After his liberation from the death camp, where he endured unimaginable torture and witnessed the death of most of those around him, Frankl went on to write and lecture about helping others by finding meaning in suffering.

The famous quote by Friedrich Nietzsche, "That which does not kill us makes us stronger,"[1] exemplifies the premise that those who've survived hardship are all the stronger because of it. Sadly, many see the flip side of this coin—the side that says they're broken, they're "no good," that they won't amount to much. This kind of negativity is infectious; too often, sufferers will hear these sentiments expressed to them or about them, and will internalize these feelings into their personal belief systems. If that describes you, challenge yourself to start seeing yourself and your potential differently—not "damaged" as a result of what's happened to you or what you've done, but *strengthened* by what you've experienced. Just surviving your painful experiences is proof that you are stronger because of them. These experiences didn't kill you; **you are still breathing, so you are still in the game.**

Dr. Lawrence Calhoun of the University of North Carolina has researched and written on the phenomenon that he calls *post-traumatic stress growth.* His research clearly suggests that personal growth can result from trauma. Dr. Calhoun emphasizes that the growth doesn't necessarily eliminate suffering; however, suffering does not have to incapacitate us, and it doesn't have to last forever.

Joyce Meyer, an international Christian speaker and author, built a worldwide ministry and became a best-selling author all while working through the pain of years of verbal, physical, and sexual abuse by her father. Rather than let her painful experiences hold her back, forcing her into a life of mediocrity or despair, Joyce Meyer's painful experiences fueled her determination to help others. Joyce Meyer Ministries, led by Joyce; her husband, Dave Meyer; and their adult children, has distributed more than 27.8 million Christian books, often in nations where Christian resources aren't readily available. They also provide care for nearly a thousand children in 35 children's homes; they've donated more than $13 million to disaster relief; they have fed more than 70,000 children at more than 650 locations throughout the world; they are involved in the rescue of women and children from human trafficking;

they provide free medical care to thousands of people through two fully funded hospitals; they have provided more than 700 water wells to provide clean drinking water in over 20 countries; and they provide help to homeless, disadvantaged youth, addicts, and the impoverished in their inner city ministries throughout the United States [2].

Others who have pushed through the feelings of pain resulting from abandonment, neglect, or abuse to accomplish great things include John Lennon of the Beatles, Supreme Court Justice Clarence Thomas; singer and actress Cher; actor and producer Sylvester Stallone; nationally known poet Maya Angelou; NFL player Dante Culpepper; NBA player Alonzo Mourning; and former United States Presidents Gerald Ford and Bill Clinton. And this is just a sampling of the more well-known individuals; there are many more who aren't famous, but who have enjoyed life after painful experiences.

Related to strength is the characteristic of determination. This is that jaw-setting, heel-digging-in quality that keeps us focused on what we want, regardless of the circumstances or the odds against us. Some people, the strong-willed among us, are born with a strong measure of determination. They are determined to have what they want, and they will try as long as they have to and do whatever needs to be done to get it.

Others appear to be born with no determination at all. They seem to float through life, with no real direction and no real desire toward any specific goal. Often described as easy-going or lazy, even these people, who seem to entirely lack ambition, can develop determination when it becomes necessary. Let us take as our example a stereotypical teenager, sent by his parents to participate in an Outward Bound program in the hopes of sparking an interest in something other than video games, drugs, girls, and parties. The Outward Bound program is founded on the four pillars of physical fitness, self-reliance, craftsmanship, and compassion, and is experienced almost entirely in a wilderness setting. Participants are put through challenges to lead them to a sense of empowerment in abilities and potential they never knew they had.

On day one of the 22-day Outward Bound course, the teen had reluctantly left the inner city of Atlanta to grudgingly participate in the program, hosted at the beautiful Table Rock Mountain in North Carolina, a place so remote that running away or refusing to participate simply aren't viable options. The boy didn't want to be there—a sentiment obvious to everyone by his words, facial expressions, and body language. But having been given no alternative, he was there. He had decided that he would show up, but nothing more.

He had no idea what the following 21 days would require of him or what they would ultimately mean in his life. On the final day of the course, a smiling, tanned, and muscular young man met with parents who almost couldn't believe what they saw. Their son, who formerly responded to them with curt one-word answers, who rarely made eye contact, and who never initiated conversation, was walking tall, talking enthusiastically (and nonstop) about all the adventures he had experienced. He told of the basic skills he had learned, from tying knots in ropes to important wilderness survival skills. He spoke of having aspirations for his future, and how the skills he had learned would be transferrable to almost any industry or setting. The parents were understandably thrilled with the transformation they saw in their son. Their son left them as a teenager who lived only in the moment, acting only for his own pleasure, and had come back an empowered young man, determined and able to create his own successful life.

The founder of Outward Bound, Kurt Hahn, has said, "There is more to us than we know. If we can be made to see it, perhaps for the rest of our lives we will be unwilling to settle for less." The motto of Outward Bound is, "To Serve, To Strive, and Not to Yield." For countless teens and adults, and over the last 50+ years of the Outward Bound programs, the founder's purpose and the organization's motto have been fulfilled, proving that the characteristics of successful survivors can, indeed, be learned—especially when one has no other alternative.

The difference between survivors and *successful* survivors is that while successful survivors do feel fear, they move forward anyway. They may feel physical or emotional pain, but they push through and keep trying. I speak from personal experience: I was in a car accident when I was younger, which left me with chronic head and neck pain for 17 long years. Physical therapy didn't help; medication lessened the pain but didn't take it away; and several orthopedic surgeons said that surgery might do more harm than good. Every day, I had to force myself to get out of bed. On top of it all, the people who caused the accident had no insurance and no way to pay for the damage they had caused.

Although I qualified for government disability payments and could have quit work and stayed home, I chose to continue working. There were days when I strongly considered the option of staying home. But for me, quitting work, staying home, and collecting a payment from the government was the equivalent of checking out of the game of life. I'm a fairly competitive person, so checking out meant throwing in the towel. I knew from my childhood days of waiting at the mailbox for the welfare check and standing in line for the "free government cheese," that if I chose that option, there would be no raises. There would be no bonuses, no opportunities for advancement, and none of that unequalled feeling of a job well done. On the days when I considered taking that seemingly easier road in life, I reminded myself of those old, clichéd sayings: "Quitters never win and winners never quit," and, "You can't win a game you're not in." Corny? I suppose so. Effective? Absolutely!

There were days when I didn't think I could stand the pain one more minute. On the worst days, I stayed home, using packs of ice to relieve the unbearable pain. But on most days, I got out of bed, put one foot in front of the other, went to work, and did my best. I functioned better on some days than others, but on the least effective days, I could at least give myself credit for getting out of bed. My choice to push through my pain led to me opening my own business and ultimately to the pain-free, peace-filled, joyful, and prosperous life I lead now. I grimace to think of the life I'd be living now had I checked out and stayed home, collecting a check from a government that was in no way responsible for the car accident that caused my pain.

Let me quickly add that there is no shame in receiving assistance— when it's *needed*. There are people who literally do not have the option of pushing through their pain, which is what government assistance is for. But it wasn't meant to be a first resort for the sort of people who are just waiting for their chance to check out; who refuse to even *try* to identify and build on their strengths.

The strength to endure difficult challenges is one of the survival skills taught to soldiers and law enforcement professionals. A soldier in combat who gives up after being wounded in battle, or a federal agent who gives up after his or her cover is blown is as good as dead. People who dig deep and garner the strength to focus on survival rather than physical or emotional pain are far more likely to make it out alive. Self-pity in combat or law enforcement will get you killed. People who have survived extreme hardship have a core of strength, something intrinsic to who they are as people. Successful survivors focus on doing whatever is necessary to reach their goals, regardless of what they feel. Through tough life experiences, they have learned to set their feelings aside and take action.

As is the case with many of the characteristics of successful survivors, that which serves as an asset one day can also be a source of problems the next. Strong people are often warriors; this can be a good thing when they're fighting a life-threatening illness, pushing their way out of a burning building, or defending themselves against a physical attacker. Those who are fighters might not have made it this far if they weren't fighters by nature. But the same attribute that may be their greatest asset can be their greatest disadvantage if they don't learn to identify which battles are worth fighting. Knowing when to push through the adversity and when to submit to the authority of another; when to allow someone else to win and when to call a draw, agreeing to disagree; all of these are crucial for ensuring that these warriors avoid locking themselves in a cycle of conflict just as damaging as obsessing over past pains.

Strong successful survivors learn that having their opinions or ideas rejected does not equate to a rejection of *them*. They know that it's important to separate their opinions, their actions, and their hopes and desires from who they are as individuals. Unless strong people separate these things, they run the risk of getting offended every time someone makes a negative comment about what they do, what they say, what they like to wear, their opinions, or their goals for the future.

Some of the battles we face in life are inconsequential when compared to our larger goals, and are best left for the opponent to score. This isn't failure; it's strategy. To use a mundane example, if you want to go see a movie but your spouse wants to stay home, regardless of whether or not you've looked forward to the movie all week or you feel you deserve your way after an exceptionally difficult week, strong successful survivors let the other person "win" by giving in on this insignificant thing, rather than fighting over it. They also don't "give in," only to spend the next few hours or days sulking! Strong successful survivors know that their peace and their good relationships are far more important than a short-lived "win."

Similarly, some battles are important to fight, but *only* when the time is right. To choose the wrong timing is to lose your advantage, and possibly the entire battle. For example, imagine you learn that your co-worker was chosen for a promotion you felt that you deserved. It's absolutely appropriate to let your boss know all the reasons why you believe you should have received the promotion, but you will get nowhere if you charge into the boss's office when he or she is busy or stressed out over other things. Patiently waiting for the right time and constructing a well thought-out case, then delivering your perspective in a calm manner is far more effective and persuasive than charging in with an emotional tirade. In other words, strong successful survivors temper their strength with patience.

Why do some people accomplish much in a day's time while others accomplish little or nothing? The root of the answer to that question lies in the choices that only we can make: primarily, the choice to feel like the strong survivor that you are, rather than feeling like a wounded victim. Playing the victim's role wastes valuable time that could be spent moving you closer to your goals. Victims often spend time telling the people around them about every perceived mistreatment, from the person who cut them off in traffic to the rude customer who just snapped at them. Playing (and remaining) the victim means too much time spent contemplating and discussing all the imagined "wrongs" that support and perpetuate victimization.

On the other hand, strong successful survivors forgive those who have hurt them, dismiss rude people, and don't waste valuable, irreplaceable time thinking about ugly events. They learn to see that it is the rude, hurtful people who have the problem. They learn to see themselves as the strong, capable, mature adults they are, pushing through adversity despite whatever negative emotions they might temporarily feel. They learn when and where to use their strength to their advantage. They learn to use all of their assets to create the lives they want to live.

But strength isn't simply a matter of conflict resolution. Related to and expressive of the characteristic of strength is empathy for others, a sense of camaraderie and respect that comes from having gone through painful experiences. On the surface, one may not think of empathy and compassion as aspects of strength; but for successful survivors, they are inextricably linked. An important facet of the strength that results from survival of trauma is a sense of empathy for victims of unfair experiences.

An example of the empathy that is borne from pain is in the life of Leigh Esau, founder and CEO of Foster CARE Closet in Lincoln, Nebraska. When Leigh was 3 years old, she was found in an abandoned apartment. No one was quite sure how long Leigh had been in there alone, but the fact that she hadn't died as a result of the freezing temperatures, or from lack of food or water was astonishing. After Leigh's rescue, she was placed into foster care and was eventually adopted. Leigh grew up, married her high school sweetheart, raised two sons, and felt led to become a foster parent. She and her husband, Patrick, loved the children placed in their care—so much so that they adopted four of them.

Time and again, Leigh and Patrick observed some of the shortcomings in the foster system. Many of their foster children arrived with only the clothing on their backs. Some arrived late at night, after the stores were closed, without shoes or appropriate clothes (that properly fit), and without coats—all of which was problematic in the cold Nebraska winters. Leigh would scrounge up something for the kids to sleep in and go shopping the following day to make sure that the children were properly dressed—and that they had the chance to feel the self-esteem that comes from wearing new, clean, and well-fitting clothes and shoes.

Leigh soon realized that many foster parents faced the same problems. She was also keenly aware that there were foster parents who couldn't or wouldn't spend their own money to provide clothes and shoes for the foster kids in their care. So Leigh decided to do something about it. She contacted managers of local stores and asked to purchase the children's clothes and shoes at the end of the season, when they were discounted for quick sale. She asked friends and neighbors for donations of gently used strollers, car seats, and other necessary items. Before long she had to rent a space to hold all the goods that had been purchased and donated. She set up a "store" where items were displayed according to gender and size, and she invited foster parents to bring foster kids in to "shop" for school clothes, winter clothes, play clothes, and summer outfits.

Leigh has seen kids, many of whom have been taken into foster care after terrible abuse, arrive at the Foster CARE Closet withdrawn, with eyes cast down, full of fear about all that's happening in their lives, only to leave later smiling, a little less afraid, with head held a little higher. For those kids who have never had new, clean clothes, the transformation is obvious to all.

Life isn't perfect for Leigh, Patrick, and their kids. Foster CARE Closet is always hoping for the support of people who care about kids who have been abandoned and abused. The work of raising four kids who were severely abused and who, as a result, have some very special needs, is a round-the-clock challenge. Working with new store managers who may or may not continue the relationships established with their predecessors is always a looming threat. Competing for donations with well-established nonprofit organizations that can afford national ad campaigns is daunting. But despite all the challenges and all the reasons for fear, sadness, and even depression, Leigh presses on, fueled by the empathy she feels for foster kids, a strength that was developed in her through her own experiences of being abandoned, and feeling unwanted and unloved.

The compassion and empathy that successful survivors have is different from sympathy. They have developed enough strength as a result of the adversities they've experienced that they can reach back to others and guide them through the steps necessary to grieve their losses and to overcome their obstacles. Strong, determined successful survivors can help others look to the future with hope. Because of this empathy, compassion, and determination to make a positive difference in the world, many successful survivors have dedicated their lives to helping others by going into helping professions like becoming psychologists, social workers, nurses, and educators.

FIVE SUCCESSFUL SURVIVAL STRATEGIES:
Strength and Determination

List at least three ways that a painful experience could have been worse. When you are ready, do this for each of your painful experiences.

Envision a goal that you would like to accomplish within the next three months. List three things that you can do in the next 24 hours to move closer to fulfilling your goal, and determine to *do* those three things. Continue your list of three action items until your goal is achieved. Do this with every goal in your life—you'll be amazed at what you can achieve!

Write a description of a "successful survivor." This can be someone you know, a made-up person, a character from a book or movie, or your future self. (If you prefer, you can draw this person or cut a picture out of a magazine of someone who looks like he or she successfully survived tough times.) This exercise will help you create a visual image of what a "successful survivor" means to you. Is this a person with a kind face? A person who walks with "swagger"? A person with a look of confidence and ambition? There is no wrong or right answer. Envision your successful survivor, and then consciously work toward becoming like that person.

Create a "T" graph with the words "strong" and "argumentative" at the top on either side of the center line of the "T." Under the word "strong," write adjectives that describe your image of the strong successful survivor. Under the word "argumentative," write adjectives that describe this type of survivor. It may help to include words that describe the way others feel around people with these characteristics. This will help you clarify the difference between being strong and argumentative. Argumentative people thwart their own success. Strong people choose their words, approach, and timing carefully, and make persuasive arguments that move them closer to achievement of their objectives.

Make a list of the types of people and/or circumstances you feel most empathetic toward. Some examples could be people who are homeless; those who live with chronic pain; children who have been orphaned; or those who have been subjected to terror, persecution, or natural disaster. Now, think of one thing you can do to help someone for whom you have genuine empathy, borne of your own experiences. Remember that "helping" can sometimes be as simple as listening or just being present.

SUMMARY

If you have experienced hardship, make sure to give yourself credit for surviving. Set your mind to refine the strength you acquired as a result of that hardship. See adversity as an opportunity for growth and a challenge to improve your life, knowing that you have the strength necessary to turn any negativity you face into a learning opportunity. Determine to thrive, answering every adversity with the knowledge that you've survived before, and you have the strength to get through your present challenges, too. Choose to remain positive, looking continually for the potential upside to every problem. This will keep your brain focused on figuring out how to turn adversity into advantage.

Decide to push through your feelings by remaining focused on what you want in life. Learn to use your strength to your advantage by choosing your battles; by being strategic about your timing; by learning to respect your relationships; by choosing peace rather than always having to be right; by learning to agree to disagree; by dismissing rejections; and by choosing never to see or speak of yourself as a victim ever again. The strength you have acquired and honed in the adversities you've experienced will serve you well in the future.

KEY POINTS FOR DEVELOPING STRENGTH

- Put the painful experiences of your life into proper perspective. You survived, and your experiences have made you stronger.
- Envision a bright future, and take steps to make it a reality.
- You may have been the victim of unfair circumstances, but the decision not to remain a victim is yours. Decide to be someone who experiences post-traumatic stress *growth*.
- Be strategic in choosing your battles and your timing. Value your peace and good relationships over "winning."
- Be determined to look for ways to use the strength and empathy developed through painful experiences to help others.

CHAPTER 2

Tenacity, Persistence, and Assertiveness

TENACIOUS AND PERSISTENT: continuing in spite of opposition, obstacles, or discouragement; never giving up

ASSERTIVE: insistent, tempered aggression

SHLEY WAS A young mom in her early 20s who was trying to care for two small children while homeless and alone. She was afraid that if the social services people knew that she and her children were homeless, they might take her children away from her. She had been in foster care herself, and she wanted desperately to avoid that for her children. She had no money and no job, but she figured that if she had a steady place to sleep and shower, she would have a better chance of finding and keeping a job. So she began to search for an apartment. Since she had no car, she and her two little children took

17

the bus from one apartment complex to another, talking to building managers about renting an apartment. Many dismissed her out of hand upon finding out that she had no money for the deposit and had no job to prove her ability to pay the rent.

Imagine the scene, as it played out again and again. Apartment managers, accusing her of wasting their time. The discouragement she must have felt, as one manager after the next told her "NO." Having to take two little children on and off the bus all day, carrying them when they could no longer walk on their own. Moving from one apartment building to the next, all day long, with no money to buy food or drinks.

After 27 different stops, spread over a period of nearly three weeks, the young mother finally persuaded an apartment manager to rent her a small apartment for less than the stated rent, to give her the first month free, and to allow her to pay the security deposit over a period of time in exchange for helping the apartment manager (who turned out to be the building owner) with a few of the tasks that the aging manager needed help with. Anyone who can be like this woman—persistent, tenacious, determined to succeed, and assertive enough to keep going when everything inside her must have been saying "quit"—will attain the goals they set for themselves in the future.

One of the characteristics shared by many successful survivors is really the combination of four closely related virtues—tenacity, persistence, determination, and assertiveness—all of which can be summed up as an indomitable spirit. This is not to say these people never get discouraged by obstacles and setbacks; they do. But unlike others, who give up when the obstacle seems too big to overcome or who just cannot bring themselves to get up and try again following a setback, successful survivors step back, reassess, make adjustments, and try again—often, again and again and again—until they obtain their desired result.

Another example of tenacity, persistence, determination, and assertiveness is found in the story of Harland Sanders, better known as "The Colonel." As the story goes, Colonel Sanders had lost his business when a major highway went in, bypassing his restaurant. At age 65, he could have sat down in his favorite chair and let depression get the best of him. It would have been natural to think: *What am I going to do? This was a raw deal. How could this have happened? I didn't do anything wrong. I've worked hard all my life, yet here I am, a failure at my age, and I'm too old to start all over.* Although he may very well have had those thoughts, he got in his car and went from restaurant to restaurant selling what he considered his greatest asset: his recipe for fried chicken.

Imagine restaurant owners looking at him like he'd lost his mind, giving him responses like, *"I use my grandmother's fried chicken recipe— it's the best. I don't need yours."* Or, *"Why in the world would I buy your recipe, when we've been using our own recipe successfully, for years. Why, everyone loves my fried chicken!"* Some politely heard him out, while others shooed him out quickly, too busy to give him even the time of day.

But because Harland Sanders refused to give up, and kept on trying, despite what he must have felt as more failure and humiliation, Kentucky Fried Chicken restaurants are now in just about every major country in the world!

When I was 15, I started working at my first real job. I was required to phone people to ask them if they would let my employer provide a comparison bid on their auto and homeowner insurance before their next insurance policy expiration. Having a job with a consistent paycheck was one of the requirements of emancipation from the child welfare system, and since there weren't many employers eagerly seeking to hire unqualified 15-year-olds, I threw myself into the work of calling people while they were trying to enjoy their dinner.

One person after the next would hang up in my ear—sometimes in anger, sometimes while I was in mid-sentence. It felt humiliating to be the person whom people most wanted to avoid. I had a long list of local residents to call, and I was always afraid of calling the home of someone with whom I went to school. I was keenly aware that most other kids at my high school were doing homework, playing sports, or hanging out with family or friends while I was annoying people with my phone calls—all because I needed a paycheck.

But despite how making phone calls made me feel, I refused to quit. I told myself that every time someone hung up on me, I was one call closer to the person who would say "YES." I motivated myself by keeping my goals in front of me and by reminding myself that I was helping those people who allowed my employer to provide an insurance quote. My immediate goal was to emancipate from the foster care system and to move out on my own, away from the abusive people and filthy environment in which I lived. On my days off, I looked for apartments and imagined a life where I could sleep without fear.

My motivation to help the people I called was one born out of a particularly painful childhood experience. When I was 8 years old, the little uninsured shack where I lived with my mentally ill grandfather and alcoholic grandmother was nearly destroyed by a fire, an accident which left us homeless and with no clothes other than those we were wearing the day of the fire. For months after the fire, we slept in the park and ate what we caught in the local lake or what food we could find in the trash cans behind grocery stores and restaurants. I wore the same dirty sundress and rubber flip-flop sandals every day, well into the winter. I was the butt of jokes, ridicule, and humiliation at school during the day and homeless at night.

So, when I was 15 and making those phone calls, I kept reminding myself that what I was doing was helping people make sure that they had appropriate insurance coverage, so that they would never experience the humiliation of homelessness as the result of an uninsured accident. Even though people were slamming the phone down or angrily telling me to never call again, my tenacity grew as I pushed myself to make those calls with a smile on my face. To avoid sounding as desperate as I was, I kept a small mirror on my desk. Even though I was talking to people on the phone and not in person, I learned that a smile "shows through" over the phone. People sense when you're friendly and sincere.

I learned to be assertive about the important issue of having appropriate insurance coverage. It wasn't long before my smile became natural, and the number of people who wanted a comparison bid began to grow. After a few months of making these calls day after day, my persistence paid off—my boss informed me that I had the highest "hit ratio" of appointments for calls nationwide!

My willingness to make the calls, my success in bringing in new business and my eagerness to learn to do anything else I was asked to do earned the respect of the man who had hired me. With every successful call and every earned paycheck, my self-esteem grew. It wasn't long before the judge granted my emancipation, and I moved out on my own. I attended high school in the morning, went to work in the afternoon, and to the local community college at night.

It wasn't long before my boss encouraged me to get my own insurance license. The tenacity I developed in making those calls has been valuable many times in my life, but none as significant as when I first applied to take the insurance license examination. I was 17, and I was turned down because the minimum age was 18. But I had been granted emancipation, and was legally considered an adult, so my boss suggested that I ask for an exception. With my boss's encouragement, I wrote to the insurance commissioner, but again was promptly turned down. I sent in several more requests until finally the commissioner must have grown weary of hearing from me. I suspect that he granted my request to test for my license just so I would stop bugging him! I passed that test and became the youngest licensed insurance agent in California, and launched a career that would carry me through my entire life—all because my first job taught me the valuable qualities of tenacity, persistence, and assertiveness.

Persistent, assertive successful survivors have made it through tough situations before, and they can make it through whatever comes their way. This is not arrogance, but is rather the confidence that comes only from successfully making it through difficulties. Living through painful experiences proves, both to oneself and to others, that they can meet any challenge and survive any adversity. As a result, they do not give up easily.

A great example of assertiveness is the story of Christy Pallos Topper, a woman looking to get into the dental hygiene program at the prestigious University of Southern California. Although she had the academic qualifications for enrollment, the deadline for applications was long past. Students had matriculated, and classes were full. Most other people would have resigned themselves to wait until the following year to enroll. But Christy didn't want to wait a year before beginning to work toward her goal, so she called the Office of the Dean and requested a meeting. She persisted until the Dean of USC's School of Dentistry agreed to a meeting. Before the meeting was over, an exception was made; Christy was accepted into USC and was added to all the right classes within days.

Determined, assertive successful survivors ask for what they want. The answer may not be what they hoped for, but they are willing to take that risk. They know that they aren't going to be any worse off for having received a negative answer than they were before. Many assertive people actually hear "no" as "not yet!" They take a negative answer as a challenge, reassess the situation, and come back with another approach.

Assertive successful survivors ask for exceptions to the rules, not in the hopes that others will take pity on them, but by communicating persuasively what's in it for the other person. For example, when I was 21, I called the owner of the most well-respected insurance agency in my area and told him boldly that I had something he needed. I told him what I believed I could do for his company as an employee. I didn't tell the owner that I was an unemployed single mom with no money for food or rent who desperately needed a job (although all that was true). My personal needs were no one else's business and were completely irrelevant to the business owner. In fact, the only thing relevant to him was how I could contribute to the efficiency and profitability of his company. Within an hour, I had a job—a job that had not been posted as available, because it had not existed before my call!

Tenacious, assertive successful survivors ask for what they want—even when there is no apparent benefit to the other person. Just before my daughter turned 21, I wrote to celebrities, politicians, professional athletes, well-known business executives, and religious leaders, asking them what advice *they* would give to a young person turning 21. I stuffed hundreds of letters into hundreds of envelopes, along with a blank card and a self-addressed, stamped envelope for the recipient to write his or her advice and send it back.

For the first week or so, I received no responses at all. The cost of the whole project was over $300, and at first it appeared as though I had wasted my money. Then the envelopes and packages began to arrive. The mail carrier looked curiously up the driveway as, day after day, he delivered packages from the Vatican, the White House, the Dalai Lama, Hollywood, New York City, and every place in between. Not only did I receive handwritten cards from former presidents, famous actors, and accomplished athletes, I received signed photographs and some excellent advice to give to my daughter. The advice she received ranged from the practical ("Don't go into debt," from former Lakers star Rick Fox) to the philosophical ("Devote your life to the greater good," from former U.S. Vice President Dick Cheney). The point is that my assertiveness in approaching these complete strangers paid off in a priceless gift that my daughter will never forget.

One common thread in the lives of all tenacious, persistent, and assertive people is that they **ask "how" questions rather than "why" questions**. In other words, successful survivors don't waste time with questions like:

"Why did this happen to me?"

"Why can't I catch a break?"

"Why does it seem like everyone has better luck than I do?"

"Why am I always the one…

...to get hurt?

...to be fired?

...to be rejected?"

Rather, tenacious, persistent, assertive people ask questions like:

"How can I fix this?"

"How can this situation improve?"

"What went wrong, and how can I prevent it from happening again?"

Take note of the kinds of questions you ask yourself. When you ask rhetorical questions that have no real answer, your brain cycles through the problem over and over again. On the other hand, when you ask the *right* questions, your brain goes to work to find answers.

FIVE SUCCESSFUL SURVIVAL STRATEGIES:
Tenacity, Persistence, and Assertiveness

Consider a desire or goal that you have given up on. If the desire or goal is part of the life you would like to live, resurrect it. Do the research necessary to determine what it will take to make your goal a reality. Then, create a step-by-step action list of what you will have to do to live your goal or desired life. If the old goal or desire is no longer a part of the future you'd like to have, think of a new goal that *would* serve your future. Do your research and create your action steps for it. Regardless of what you choose as a desire or goal, set your mind to *do* the steps needed to make it a reality, and never, *ever* entertain the possibility of giving up.

Think of at least one thing you need that could improve your life within the next 30 days. Next, make a list of the people or organizations you could approach who are in a position to provide what you need. For each of the people or organizations on your list, think of at least one way that helping you would also help them, or move them closer toward the achievement of their goal. If you cannot think of a single way that the other party would benefit from helping you, ask yourself what the other party needs or wants that you might be able to provide or do for them. If all else fails, try asking them directly how you can be of service to them. You will be pleasantly surprised at what you can very easily do for someone that will still be extremely useful to them. For example, if you plan on approaching a company, search online for articles, press releases, and newsletters that may give some insight into initiatives they hope to accomplish or challenges they face. Once you have some ideas on what they may need, call, email, or write to ask for an appointment to speak to them about a mutually beneficial opportunity. Be sure to follow up by phone within three business days of your initial approach.

Decide ahead of time to refuse to take offense to anything that is said or done by people you approach with your proposals or projects. Determine to see anything like a rejection or objection as the other person simply not having enough of a reason or enough information (yet) to make an affirmative decision. Before you make your follow-up call or go to an in-person meeting, practice responding to anticipated objections. (Don't scoff at this! No one communicates perfectly the first time.) If you're not sure what objections may arise or how to best respond to them, consider doing an online search of responses to common objections. You may have to search for a time until you find responses that are appropriate to you and your proposal, and which are consistent with your style. Once you find some responses that feel right to you, practice responding to objections you think you may hear until you are comfortable, even confident, in countering them.

Search in movies, television, and online for people who look persistent and assertive. Study their facial expressions, body language, the way they tilt their heads, and any other details you can glean: their appearance, the way they speak, the words they use, the way they behave, anything. Once you have an idea of how these people behave, try acting the way they act. It may feel disingenuous and uncomfortable at first, but the more you practice persistently asking for what you want, the more normal it will feel. You *can* train yourself to be tenacious, persistent, and assertive.

When you are tempted to ask someone a question that starts with the word "why," *stop.* Take the time to reconstruct the sentence so that it begins with the words "how" or "what." For example, change "Why are you always late?" to "What would have to happen for you to be on time?" or "How could you rearrange your responsibilities so that you would be on time in the future?"

SUMMARY

If you don't ask, you will not receive. Understand that there will be discomfort in some of the things you'll have to do before you attain personal and professional success. There is work involved in every worthy gain. Just remember that any discomfort is temporary, and it can pay off in big ways.

There are some things you can do that will help you to become more tenacious, persistent, and assertive. First, look at the purpose behind what you're being asked to do. Find ways that the task at hand can be helpful to others by thinking about who will be helped, or how life might be more difficult if the task is left undone. Even when the last thing you feel like doing is smiling, do it anyway. You can change your attitude for the better simply by adopting the facial expressions and body language you would have if you felt naturally happy. When you do that, opportunities are far more likely to present themselves. Think about it—if you had a great idea for a new business but needed a partner, would you approach someone who seemed unhappy, frustrated, or who gave up easily? Of course not—you would find someone who is cheerful, persistent, assertive, and determined to succeed (we'll talk more about optimism in the next chapter).

If you are assertive enough to ask, tenacious enough to keep trying, and determined enough to never give up, eventually you will get what you are hoping for—or you may get something even better!

KEY POINTS FOR DEVELOPING TENACITY, PERSISTENCE, AND ASSERTIVENESS

- Decide to have an indomitable spirit—to never, ever give up.
- Ask for what you want, and tell the person you're asking what he or she will gain by responding in the affirmative.
- Hear "No" as "Not yet!" Gather data, reassess the circumstances, and come back with another approach.
- Adopt a hope-filled attitude of expectancy; "act" like you have everything together until it becomes a reality. People are far more likely to give you a shot if your demeanor is hopeful and confident.
- Replace "why" questions with "how" and "what" questions. Let your brain go to work for you in finding actionable answers.

CHAPTER 3

Optimism and Positivity

OPTIMISTIC AND POSITIVE: choosing a favorable view of events or conditions and expecting a favorable outcome

RESIST DEPRESSION: actively fighting the temptation to become negative, depressed, or oppressed

---

FORMER U.S. REP. Patrick J. Kennedy first noticed the signs of his depression at 13. In various interviews, he has openly talked about self-medicating with marijuana, alcohol, and cocaine. By age 17, this future leader was hospitalized for addiction.

The youngest son of Sen. Edward M. "Ted" Kennedy and nephew of assassinated former President John F. Kennedy and assassinated Sen. Robert F. Kennedy, Patrick was raised by a father who suffered from what would now likely be diagnosed as PTSD. The effects of his father having seen two of his brothers murdered resulted in him being startled by loud noises. He felt driven to keep himself busy constantly, and is said to have self-medicated with alcohol. While his mother was loving and supportive, Patrick has said that she too struggled with depression and alcoholism.

Being part of a nationally known family, the stories of their family tragedies are often rehashed in the media. It seemed there was nowhere Patrick could go to get away from the constant reminder of the tragedies the family had endured. Diagnosed as bipolar II, it looked as though Patrick was on the path to a life of depression and sadness.

As it turned out, Patrick Kennedy's life is nothing like that dismal prediction. He is happily married, has a beautiful family, and is an avid advocate for brain research and good mental health services. He works tirelessly to eliminate the stigma of mental illness and its treatments, and works in support of legislation requiring insurance companies to provide coverage for mental illness in the same way that they do for medical conditions. Patrick attributes the turnaround in his life to several things, including the hard work of a mentor who saw the potential in him and invested the time needed to get Patrick to see it for himself; regular attendance at a 12-step recovery program; regular exercise; and getting enough sleep.

Sadly, many people can't imagine looking beyond their present, depressing circumstances to a brighter future. Depression is like a deep hole, one that is easy to fall into and hard to escape. Even the efforts required to avoid falling into the hole (or climbing out of it) is work. It is anything but passive; it requires deliberate effort. And worst of all, it's when you least feel like making that effort that it is most needed. The actions involved in resisting depression are myriad, but the most significant is a connectedness to others. At times when those struggling with sadness are most likely to withdraw, the best thing they can do is to spend time with others.

Optimism and positive thinking often don't come naturally to survivors of trauma. Victims of violent crimes, for example, often lose their optimistic outlook and sense of safety, along with everything else their perpetrator took from them. But, as in the case of Patrick Kennedy, survivors can *intentionally choose* to have hope for their future. They can carefully rebuild their optimism, adopting a positive outlook on life and having favorable expectations for the future—which, while it may require more effort for some than for others, *can be done*.

One psychiatrist who did a great deal of work in the area of depression and resiliency is Dr. Frederic Flach. Dr. Flach had an interesting approach to depression, one which was well ahead of his time. Rather than work to keep a patient from feeling depressed, he would gently empower the patient to work *through* a process that he termed, "a cycle of falling apart and subsequently putting the pieces of our lives together again in a new form." Dr. Flach considered this process of falling apart and reassembling the pieces of our lives into a "new normal" as an expected and recurring theme throughout the human life cycle—something natural, rather than something to be avoided.

Dr. Flach found that "falling apart" is often the quickest way to a resilient "bounce back" after a setback. I would suggest that, when it comes to the process of "falling apart," rather than spending the energy to try to avoid it, you can use it as a "set-up" for a resilient recovery—not back into the way things used to be, but into a new and improved life.

An example of this can be found in the life of Esther Harrington. Esther was a good girl from a good family, who found herself away from home and family for the first time as she and her best friend entered college. She had always followed the rules: never missed a curfew; never disrespected her parents; and faithfully attended church. When some classmates from college invited Esther and her best friend to drive a great distance across the state line to a party, they thought it would be a fun thing to do. They suspected there would be alcohol and boys, and they knew that their parents would not approve of them driving that distance, so neither of the girls told their families what they were planning to do.

Acting against the rules (and totally out of character for them), the young girls decided to join in the fun and go to the party. They had fun at the party and thought they were "home-free;" that they'd never have to tell their parents what they'd done. After all, neither girl got drunk; they didn't do anything inappropriate. It wasn't that big of a deal…that is, until they were on the highway driving back.

Another friend who had also gone to the party was driving, Esther's best friend was in the passenger seat, and Esther herself was curled up asleep in the backseat when suddenly a pickup truck going the other direction tried to make an un-signaled left turn. The driver of the pickup was drunk, and had misjudged the turn. Rather than turning in front of them, he turned right into them.

The pickup truck driver was trying to turn into a convenience store. Thankfully, there were a couple of people there who immediately ran out when they heard the noise of the crash. They were able to pull Esther's friend and the driver out of the car to the side of the road. They thought they were done, and as they watched the fuel drain out of the punctured gas tank, Esther's friend sat looking around in a daze, seeing nothing in particular, until she heard someone say, "Look at that gas pour out onto the pavement. The car is going to blow." She could hardly move—she didn't realize at the time how badly hurt she was from all the injuries she'd incurred—but she tried to turn to her right and left to find Esther. When she realized that Esther wasn't there, she called out to the people surrounding her that her best friend was in the backseat. They told her that no one else was in the car. She begged them to go look again, and sure enough, they found Esther unconscious, pinned on the floor of the car between the front and rear seats. They had to tear the car apart, literally, to get her out, but they were able to do so not long before the little car they had been in exploded into flames.

For a year following the accident, Esther Harrington had to endure surgeries, physical therapy, and excruciating pain as she tried to recover from a broken back, broken arm, other broken bones and multiple lacerations on her face. For much of that time, a complete recovery seemed nearly impossible. In fact, well-meaning people tried to prepare Esther for what they thought was inevitable and irreparable—facial deformation and severe physical limitations for the rest of her life. As her friends went on with their lives, moving toward their bright futures, Esther lived in constant pain, slowly trying to conquer each day, one at a time.

There were a lot of dark and lonely days. Friends didn't know what to say or where to look when making conversation, so many of them stopped calling and visiting. When Esther was out in public, people would look at her face and quickly look away. Some people awkwardly stared, probably trying to figure out what had happened to her. One woman came up to Esther in a department store and very boldly asked her, "Your face looks so *bad*—what on earth *happened* to you?!"

Esther had been a very outgoing, vibrant, pretty girl, and her beauty was inextricably woven into the fabric of her identity. Now, she was no longer a pretty girl. At the age of 17, Esther found herself considering her worth and value and identity apart from physical appearance. She found that it helped her to be able to laugh at herself and her circumstances. She learned that her good nature and sense of humor seemed to put people at ease. She learned to give people grace by assuming that their awkward behavior and rude words were well-intentioned. Ultimately, she learned to look beyond the surface of people to see their quiet struggles. She became especially sensitive to those who were withdrawn or lonely, and became determined to befriend them.

Throughout her journey toward her "new normal," Esther developed a gratitude for the fact that she had survived the accident. She was keenly aware that she had been just "a breath away," as she puts it, from leaving this life. She learned that physical beauty is fleeting, and that it is what's inside of each person that is important. She learned that she had no choice but to persevere if she was going to get through this challenge successfully. She believed that God had spared her because He had a purpose for her life, and Esther was determined to find it.

Rather than focus on what she had lost or what could have been, Esther's optimism—her determined resistance against letting depression drag her down—allowed her to draw strength from having been spared from death. She knew that there must be a purpose yet for her to fulfill. She was able to find peace by letting go of what was behind her. Rather than marinating in the guilt of a poor choice or dwelling on what might have been in her future had she not gone to that party and been in that accident, Esther focused solely on whatever new normal would result from her hard work of moving forward.

Esther credits her faith, her positive attitude, supportive family, and excellent medical care for her complete recovery. Her recovery was so complete, in fact, that if you hadn't heard her story, you would never guess that she had ever endured facial reconstruction surgery, or any of the other injuries and surgeries and months of painful struggle. Esther Harrington is a beautiful woman, inside and out, and is happily married with a wonderful family.

To Dr. Flach's point, Esther did not go back to being the person she was before the accident. Rather, she came through her experiences as a person grateful to be alive, with a greater empathy for others than she might ever have found if she hadn't gone through the process of "falling apart." Esther let go of the past and the expectations that went along with it. No longer was she the young girl who considered physical appearance to be the core of her worth and value. With her newly plumbed depth of appreciation for life, Esther built a new life, richer than what she'd had previously.

When I was in my early 20s, living paycheck to paycheck while trying to earn enough money to pay rent and buy food for my little girl and myself, I fought against depression every day. There were a million reasons for me to be depressed: I had no family, no money, and no safety net. I wore the same two outfits to work day after day. My little girl seemed to continually need things that I could not provide. We couldn't afford to go anywhere, or do anything. We lived on beans and rice, ramen noodles, peanut butter, and macaroni and cheese. I was driving an unreliable car, and seemed to always be just one breakdown away from not having a way to get to and from work. To make matters worse, I was working in a male-dominated office (and industry) where I was paid less than men who did the same job. Because I had gone from customer service to sales, and knew how to do my own service work, I was also expected to do all my own clerical work, while my male counterparts had secretaries.

It would have been easy to be depressed, and to let that depression slide into despair. I fought depression by writing notes to myself that encouraged me to keep trying, to work harder than my competition, and to refuse to give up. I taped notes to my bathroom mirror and pinned them on the walls of my office cubicle. In fact, I still have the paper that hung in my cubicle for six and a half years, until the day I took it down and packed it up as I left that job to open my own company. That note included the following quotes:

"If you believe, you will receive whatever you ask for in prayer."
—Jesus

"Whatever the mind of man can conceive and believe, it can achieve."
—Napoleon Hill

"Our duty, as men and women, is to proceed as if limits to our ability did not exist. We are collaborators in creation."
—Pierre Teilhard de Chardin

"There is nothing capricious in nature, and the implanting of a desire indicates that its gratification is in the constitution of the creature that feels it."
—Ralph Waldo Emerson

"Whether you think you can, or you think you can't, you're right!"
—Henry Ford

The paper that hung on my bathroom mirror said:

Whenever I have a thought of limitation, I replace it with a vision of my achievement!

In addition to the little written notes I used to encourage myself, I would cut pictures out of magazines of the things we needed or that I hoped to have one day and tape them to my bathroom mirror. Sometimes, it would seem to take forever to reach a goal. But with every little success, I'd be more willing to drag myself out of bed rather than sleep my way through a bout of depression. With my little girl depending on me, I knew I didn't have the luxury of indulging those feelings of depression.

People who choose to have a positive attitude don't blame others, even when their current circumstances are the direct result of someone else's actions or failure to act. Optimistic survivors know that their circumstances don't improve by placing blame on someone else. **Placing blame implies that someone else is in charge of our lives.** In fact, the very act of blaming others for the circumstances we face puts us in the position of being seemingly helpless victims, which opens the door to self-pity and depression. Seeing oneself that way influences the choices we make, the risks we take (or avoid), and the outcomes we get in our lives.

Optimistic people, on the other hand, take charge of their circumstances, however dire those circumstances may be. People who deliberately choose a positive outlook see problems as challenges to overcome and opportunities to grow. They see themselves as conquering the challenges they face; they are victors who have overcome (or are in the process of overcoming) ugly circumstances, and who will thrive because of the coping mechanisms forged through adversity. And this is a choice that anyone can make: choosing to think and act like an optimist means not focusing on the adversities endured, or what's missing, or what others are doing to you or not doing for you. It's a choice to live in the present, press toward the future, and let go of the past.

Opening the door to depression is dangerous. Depression grows like mold, thriving in cold, dark places. It soon permeates every aspect of life until it destroys positivity and optimism. Optimistic successful survivors resist the temptation to entertain feelings of depression—even for a few moments. Notice that I do not say that they don't *ever* feel sad, depressed, oppressed, frustrated, or pessimistic; they do. In fact, if anyone ever earned the right to throw a full-blown pity party, it's someone who has suffered at a time when they were unable or too vulnerable to prevent it. But just because they have earned the *right* to indulge in self-pity, doesn't mean they *should*. Self-pity results in pessimism and depression, which only exacerbates the problems they're facing. Self-pity and "woe-is-me" thinking should be avoided at all costs: **indulging, even briefly, in self-pity is like taking a taste of poison; it will make you feel worse, and it may even kill you.**

Successful survivors learn how to proactively fight depression. Although this sounds like an over-simplification of a complicated issue, successful survivors know that if they give in to depression and fail to take care of themselves, there is no one who can rescue them. They know that indulging thoughts of depression for even a few moments can lead to a half hour, a half hour can lead to a day, and days can turn into weeks. Life is too short to give in to depression; to spend time wishing things were different or thinking about how things used to be or should be now is to waste time that you can never get back. You get the same amount of time every day as everyone else does; what you *do* with yours is the only thing that will determine your success. Using time wisely is an investment that will reap a return in your future.

Successful soldiers remind themselves of previous victories before going into battle. For successful survivors, the fight against depression can be fought and won in the same way—by reminding themselves how they previously overcame adversity. A powerful weapon to help people do this is to create what my friend and mentor H.H. "Corky" Kindsvater, MSW, author of *Restoring Childhood*, calls a *Lifebook*. This can be a book with written stories, photos, poems, newspaper articles, magazine cut-outs, or drawings—whatever it takes to encourage you and remind you of the challenges you've overcome, the accomplishments you've achieved, the people you've helped, the relationships you've developed, and the goals you have for your future. A *Lifebook* reminds you that tough situations don't last forever; you've made it through other difficulties, and you'll make it through your present challenges too. Chapter 9 will walk you through the steps of creating your own Lifebook.

Having clearly defined goals for the life you want to live can be a powerful tool in motivating you and in helping to put your life in the proper perspective. There are people and situations in all of our lives that can trigger the feelings of sadness or frustration that lead to depression. Your goals help you turn your attention from those "triggers"—the irritating neighbor or co-worker who is not a permanent part of your life—toward the future you want for yourself. Proper perspective reminds you that the young children who require a lot of your time will eventually grow up; that the long hours of homework required for your education will be a thing of the past once you've earned your degree; and that whatever problems you're facing now are temporary.

The first step in actively fighting depression is to identify your personal "triggers." Typical triggers include birthdays and holidays; exhaustion; the crash after eating sugar; illness and pain; interaction with people who push your buttons; and sad events, such as the end of a relationship or the death of a loved one. You may find that a certain song or a familiar perfume can trigger sadness. Some people discover allergies to certain foods cause their depression. You may already know some of your triggers, but journaling or creating a spreadsheet to keep track of your activities and feelings can help you connect the dots between your triggers and times when you feel sadness or despair. This kind of record can *also* help you to find the connections between your "good triggers" and the feelings of joy or contentedness that follow. Once you know your triggers, you are better able to avoid or diminish the triggers to negative emotions, and take intentional steps to choose the triggers that result in positive emotions.

Many victims of trauma spend years fighting depression. They have what seems like hundreds of triggers. They feel like puppets being manipulated by an evil puppeteer. I know, because I used to be one of them; for years before I learned that I could proactively fight depression, I was subject to a seemingly endless series of negative triggers. For example, if I had contact with someone who happened to have the same name as my mother, I would plunge into a funk, wondering what she was doing, whom she was with, if there was any chance she ever thought about me, and if she cared at all about what was going on in my life. Another trigger was my birthday; a full month before my birthday, I'd start hoping that *this* would be the year I'd get cards from my mother or father. I'd build myself up so much that the inevitably empty mailbox on my birthday would have the power to destroy the good wishes that came from anyone else.

Like a pilot who sees a potential mid-air collision and takes corrective action to avert disaster, successful survivors pay attention to what precedes their feelings of depression, so that they can take precautionary, proactive measures in the future. They avoid people and places that they know lead to sadness. Because I knew that my birthday was a trigger for depression, rather than waiting to see who remembered my birthday and being disappointed by those who hadn't, I learned to make my own plans for lunches with friends, for trips, and for other enjoyable activities on that day. I chose not to gauge my happiness by those who didn't remember my birthday, but by those precious people who did.

Another common trigger for depression is the feeling of being overwhelmed that comes from facing multiple challenges at the same time. For example, if you don't have enough money to make it through the month and don't know how you are going to pay bills and put food on the table, having the extra expense of a flat tire can throw you into a feeling of being overwhelmed. And that overwhelmed feeling is easily exacerbated by the demands of your job, family, or otherwise manageable challenges.

It's even easier to become overwhelmed when there is physical pain involved. Pain can make it difficult to think clearly and to accomplish the unfinished tasks before you. Financial issues compound other challenges, because it's difficult to find solutions to problems if you're hungry and homeless, or if you don't have the money to rectify those huge issues. It's not as though successful survivors never feel overwhelmed. They do. But they've learned that in order to successfully navigate through multiple challenges, they must break them down, prioritize them, and deal with one issue at a time.

To avoid the feelings of depression brought on by being overwhelmed, it is especially important not to exaggerate the facts, and to not speculate on what tomorrow may bring. Take each problem individually and try to think dispassionately about all the possible solutions, regardless of how implausible or even ridiculous they may sound. Try to be objective: Imagine that you are giving advice to a friend who is faced with your circumstances. Focusing on how to find possible solutions shifts your mind from pessimism to cautious optimism, from feeling hopeless to hopeful. This shift in attitude is integral to finding the resolutions you seek.

Once you've written out as many possible solutions as you can think of, give yourself a break. Resist the temptation to give in to the sense of being overwhelmed or depressed by taking some simple steps to control something that *is* within your control, like taking a shower and putting on clean clothes. Do your hair; ladies, put on make-up. It *will* make you feel better. Taking control of even the most mundane thing can help you move toward a more hopeful feeling. It will also help you become prepared for a break—what some call luck. But successful survivors create their own luck by being prepared and looking for opportunities.

Optimistic successful survivors know that successful outcomes are the result of preparation, hard work, and expectation that good things are in their future.

Success = (preparation + hard work) x positive expectations

Optimistic successful survivors intentionally look for someone to help, even when they themselves feel down. Although it may sound counter-intuitive to reach out to help someone else when you're struggling, it can be the most helpful thing you can do for yourself. Once you've done all you can do to resolve the challenges you face, the process of helping someone else serves to get your focus off yourself and your problems and onto someone else. This helps you gain perspective. It engages your assets—the strengths, talents, and abilities in you that can be helpful to others. **Finding someone to help rather than trying to find someone to help you is a powerful way to proactively fight depression.**

I am not suggesting that you never seek help; by all means, do as Patrick Kennedy did: find a mentor, attend a 12-step program, exercise, get plenty of sleep, drink plenty of water, and eat healthy foods. But when you are in the midst of a potentially overwhelming situation, helping someone else can be extremely valuable in getting your mind off your own situation for a time. It's also often true that in the process of helping someone else, you stumble upon a solution or resource for improving your own circumstances.

Whether you tend toward feelings of depression or not, one sure-fire way to feel sad is to think about what you don't have, dwelling on times when you have been mistreated, or when you knew you weren't wanted or loved. As simplistic as it may sound, optimistic successful survivors learn to avoid these thoughts and the depression that usually accompanies them.

Some people are naturally able to deliberately choose what they are going to think about. When a negative thought comes to mind, they are able to immediately notice it and replace it with a positive thought. Others find themselves prisoners of their negative thoughts. Their imagination runs wild with all the terrible things that could happen. They are sadly unaware that they can "change the channel" of their minds, and choose what they think about.

Every single one of us can train our minds to take negative thoughts "captive," replacing them with positive thoughts. We can intentionally do the work that cultivates a positive attitude. One way to train yourself to avoid negative thinking is to wear a rubber band around your wrist, snapping it every time you catch yourself having a negative thought. It's a free, simple, and effective tool to begin the process of reprogramming your mind to avoid negativity.

Once negative thoughts are arrested, the next step is to intentionally replace them with positive, optimistic and hopeful thoughts; it really is like changing the channel on the television. To do this effectively, collect thoughts, pictures, jokes, or whatever it is that makes you smile or laugh. These can be photographs that remind you of good times, pictures cut out of magazines of places you'd like to go or things you'd like to have, funny or inspiring videos, or stories. Intentionally positive survivors have these things ready, so that when a negative thought comes to mind, they can instantly replace it with a thought that lifts their spirits.

Successful survivors focus on what they have (their good qualities and characteristics), what they are striving for (their goals), and how they are going to reach their goals (their plans). They replace thoughts of people who have harmed them with thoughts of good, safe people in their future who can be trusted. Successful survivors replace ugly scenes in their mind with a picture of a beautiful place they hope to see, a home they plan to have, or images of the lives they want to live.

This visualization of lifestyles and places is even easier now than ever before, thanks to the Internet. You can search for images of places you want to visit, homes you would like to live in, and the things you would like to have or do. When you look at images and imagine yourself in the picture, you are planting these pictures firmly in your mind so that you can easily recall them to replace negative thoughts and ugly images. The more you recall these images, the more likely you are to recognize them when they show up in your life!

It's important to note that, during this process of visualizing a happier future, you do not allow yourself to negatively compare your goals and dreams to everything you currently lack. Don't let your inspirations for the future turn into criticisms of your present—these are more than empty goals, these are things that you can and *will* have in the future. Let these hope-filled, positive visualizations lift you upward and onward.

Optimistic successful survivors don't buy the excuses that pessimistic people typically use to dismiss their negative attitudes. Some common excuses are:

"I'm just being realistic."

"You're overlooking the facts and being a 'Pollyanna.'"

"If I don't expect good things to happen, then I won't be disappointed when they don't."

The facts may be ugly, but you don't have to base your outlook on the facts as they currently stand. Facts can change in an instant; for example, it may be a fact that you've received no responses to your job applications, but you could hear back from multiple companies within the next 24 hours! Suddenly, the facts have changed; where once there was nothing, there are now a number of opportunities.

In situations where the facts cannot be so easily changed, such as the case of the death of a loved one, successful survivors can still benefit from revisiting their *Lifebook*, reminding themselves that they have lived through painful situations before and that there is still a bright future for their lives. So long as you are still breathing, you're still in the game of life. Give yourself permission to create and work toward the goals you hold for your future. This deliberate shift from contemplation of the pain you feel to contemplation of a good future is the very thing that will help you to regain some happiness.

For example, imagine a wife whose husband leaves her for another woman. Suddenly, she is alone. She didn't plan on this, and of course there is shock, anger, sadness, grief—along with feelings of abandonment and betrayal. Eventually, as an acceptance of her new reality sets in, she has a choice to make. She can live in perpetual anger and sadness, or she can decide to take charge of her life and choose to adopt an optimistic outlook for her future. Which decision is more likely to lead to meeting someone new, falling in love, and being happy again? It's clear that optimism is far more attractive than anger, sadness, and bitterness.

But how do you choose optimism when your world has fallen apart? You deliberately replace ugly thoughts with beautiful ones; you refuse to speak negative words, instead choosing positive, hopeful words. Words are more powerful than most people can imagine. The wrong words spoken can get you fired, arrested, and can even lead to your loved ones ending your relationship. Negative words can even nudge someone toward committing suicide, or can provoke someone to commit homicide.

Meanwhile, the right words said to the right people at the right time can get you the job, the promotion, the raise; they can lead to friendship or marriage, get you started in a business, get you the loan, help you buy the house, or help your doctor properly diagnose and treat an illness. In short, the right words can mean the difference between life and death.

The sooner you really start believing that your words are powerful, the closer you will be to living the life you want to live. I'm not talking about repeating positive-sounding phrases or some kind of new-age hocus pocus. I'm referring to the very real power that you have to improve or destroy your life through the common conversations you have every day. The greatest tool you have, which can ignite (or extinguish) the power within you to change your life, is right under your nose!

The things you say are windows straight into your mind, your heart, and your soul. You may never have thought of it this way, but consider this for a moment: if someone makes a racially prejudiced remark, everyone within hearing distance instantly gets a glimpse into how that person "really feels" about the race of people he or she just insulted. People often try to dismiss hurtful or poorly chosen words by saying, "I was just kidding" or "I didn't mean it." But what comes out of a person's mouth is an insight into that person's true mindset or feelings, and is more often than not a fairly accurate reflection of the person. It has been said that when a person shows you who they really are through their words or actions, believe them. Let's be mindful that, although you may never say a word to them, the people around you are making judgments about you based on your words and behaviors.

So, what must you do to improve your relationships, your career, and your life? Speak *only* what you want to be known for and only what you want to have in your life. If you have a tendency to repeat things that others in your family or circle of friends say, but these things don't reflect (or no longer reflect) who you truly are or how you think, decide today to consider your words before speaking and to stop saying those things that don't accurately reflect your true self and the future you want to have.

This is something I had to work at for years. I was raised by a very negative man and a very superstitious woman. He was always predicting failure and what he called "bad luck," and she was always predicting some negative event that was somehow mysteriously tied to the random crossing of our path by a black cat or one of us having walked under a ladder, or some other such nonsense. For years into my adulthood, I unthinkingly repeated the babble these two had spouted. It wasn't until I determined to take note of the words I spoke that I realized what a negative, superstitious fool I must have sounded like. When I began to deliberately choose the words that best represented the person I wanted to be, my attitude began to change, opportunities began to show up, and my circumstances began to improve.

When the negative person says, "What if I lose my job?", his or her imagination conjures up pictures of being destitute. When the positive person says, "What if I lose my job?", he or she begins to consider new and better jobs, or a business that could be started, or a pivot into a completely different career or lifestyle after being released from the responsibility of present employment.

Negative people say, "Why, oh why?"

Positive people, the optimistic successful survivors of trauma, say, "Why not?"

Shawn Achor, in his book *The Happiness Advantage*, talks about a study done at Harvard University, where participants were asked to envision themselves in the scenario of being in a bank at the time of a robbery. In the act of robbing the bank, the bank robber shoots the participant in the arm and runs out of the bank. The participants were then asked how they felt about the situation. Those with a negative mindset bemoaned the fact that they were in the wrong place at the wrong time. They saw the situation as a terrible, traumatic event that would go down in their history as one of the worst things that happened in their lives. Those with a positive mindset expressed gratitude that the shot fired didn't hit them in the head or heart and kill them instantly. The positive survivors of the traumatic event were grateful to have lived through the traumatic experience with only a wound to the arm, one that would not prohibit them from recovering fully and going on to lead a rewarding life.

Think about the participants of this study. Which ones would you rather be in relationship with? Which would you rather work with? Which would you rather start a business with? Which would you rather have around in a time of need? People who intend to deliberately create good lives for themselves know to surround themselves with these sorts of positive people, those who have an attitude of gratitude. People with a positive outlook tend to smile more, laugh more, and generally enjoy life more. People with a negative outlook tend to gravitate toward feelings of frustration, sadness, or cynicism.

Pay special attention to the words that come out your mouth. If you have a habit of saying negative things like, "It's just my luck" or, "Without bad luck I'd have none at all," or some other negative thing, work to intentionally remove these kinds of statements from your vocabulary. They're neither positive nor uplifting. Employers, friends, co-workers, neighbors…anyone trying to intentionally surround themselves with only positive people will avoid you. And what's worse, you may never know why; people who have been avoided are often not even aware of the opportunities they have missed or the relationships that could have been. The good news is that it's never too late to adopt a positive outlook and to attract positive people into your life.

Start today by saying what you want in your life. Don't mention what you don't want, including the problems you are currently facing. Don't voice worries about something that may never happen or something that could get worse (but which could also turn out okay). Don't complain and don't gossip (even if what you have heard is true, don't pass it on). Avoid sharing unsolicited, negative opinions. (For some, this eliminates most of their daily conversations!)

Speak about the challenges you are facing only to those who may be able to help you, or else to someone whom you may be able to encourage because of empathy developed by what you have been through. Sometimes people simply need to hear that someone else has overcome something similar before they believe that they can, too. Don't talk about negative things with people who can do nothing to change your circumstances. When you speak about your problems to people who are powerless to help, all you are doing is reminding yourself of your problems, thereby making those problems the focus of your life, even as you bring the other person down with you.

It's not enough to eliminate negative speech. Doing so is a good start, but to get measurably good results, you need to work to replace negative words with positive, optimistic ones. For example, don't say things like:

"I heard the company was going to lay off a bunch of people. I'll probably be one of the first to go, because I haven't been here as long as most of the others." Instead, try saying, *"If the company lays people off, I know that no matter what happens I'll be fine!"* You may be worried half to death about losing your job, but don't let those worries take control of your voice; don't let your anxieties gain control of your powerful words.

A good rule to remember is this: ***Don't let everything that pops into your head fall out of your mouth.***

Begin today by saying nothing that could reflect negatively on you, your employer, or anyone else. Say nothing that could offend or hurt someone or some group of people. Intentionally find something good to say to others and about others. As the old saying goes, if you can't find anything good to say, don't say anything at all. This may not come easily to you, but with practice it will eventually be a natural part of your day.

When you change your words from negative to positive, good opportunities that would otherwise have been missed will begin to open up to you. If you pay attention, you will soon be able look back on today as the day you chose to be positive, a personal turning point—the day you took charge and changed your life!

When actively fighting depression, sometimes you have to give yourself credit for just getting up in the morning. If the best you can do is get out of bed, do it. Establishing and maintaining a regular routine can help tremendously. Force yourself to get up and do each step of your routine. Make a list of "to-do" items, prioritize them in order of importance, and do them one at a time, starting with those of the highest importance, checking off each one as it's done. With every completed task, you'll feel a little better. When you're feeling depressed, it's important to not look at everything that needs to be done in your life as one big clump of problems. This will only serve to overwhelm you. Make sure not to skip the step of making your list of items. That way, you can look at one item at a time and avoid the sense of being overwhelmed that can accompany "clusters" of challenges.

Research has shown that exercise and deep breathing increases oxygen to the brain, which improves our ability to think and solve problems, improves creativity, and helps to alleviate feelings of depression. You don't have to become an athlete to get the blood pumping to your brain. A 20-minute walk can help, as will yoga, Pilates, swimming, dancing, or whatever else works for you.

As silly as it may sound, it can help to wash your hands in cold water, to breathe deeply, and to keep your eyes looking upward when fighting depression. Researchers have demonstrated that when your eyes are looking down, your head follows. Your shoulders slump; your "sad posture" actually leads to more feelings of sadness. The advice to "keep your head up" is substantive and realistically effective. Research has suggested that when you keep your head up and the corners of your mouth turned up into a smile, you are triggering the release of "feel good" chemicals in your brain. (And everyone who has ever tried not to cry knows that the best way to keep from crying is to look upward!)

Some people avoid a general feeling of malaise by eliminating the newspaper or the nightly news from their life. Some refrain from answering the phone, or from looking at email or texts after a set time at night, when it's too late to take action anyway and the only thing that can come of it is anxiety, depression, or loss of sleep.

Try all of these suggested actions to help you fight depression and negative attitudes. Discover what works for you, and make those actions a daily habit. You *will* see an elevation in your mood, and when you intentionally elevate your mood, you will begin to notice an improvement in your attitude and overall feelings of well-being.

Many people, at one time or another in their lives, have been diagnosed with some sort of mental health problem. The notion of a "mental health diagnosis" is a misnomer, as the mere mention of a "diagnosis" implies an unhealthy or diseased condition. Those who have been through difficult or traumatic situations may naturally exhibit the results of those experiences. That does not mean that they have to wear the label of mental illness for the rest of their lives. The average person who experiences trauma is bound to exhibit residual effects for a time.

When mental health professionals see patients, it is their responsibility to assess the information they take in and to make a mental health diagnosis, just as medical doctors do. Their role is also the same: to help the person feel better. The way they do that is by naming and categorizing the malady and prescribing appropriate therapy and/or medication. The diagnosis (label) they give patients often determines whether or not government funding or private insurance will pay for treatment. In order to make sure that patients qualify for funding for the treatment they need, some well-meaning mental health professionals will place very serious sounding labels on people—sometimes multiple labels at once. Sadly, many people receive those diagnoses as though they were a chronic and terminal illness, rather than an identification of a temporary situation. If you were diagnosed as having the flu, you wouldn't label yourself as someone who had a perpetual case of the flu. You would expect to treat it, get well, and move on.

If you have been labeled with a diagnosis, consider first that the label may not have been accurate when it was given to you. No one is perfect; determining a person's mental health is not an exact science, and because many mental health professionals only have a brief amount of time to see each patient, it is quite possible that you were misdiagnosed, or that the characteristics of the diagnosis weren't adequately explained to you. If you were young when diagnosed, take into consideration that you were still developing. What's true for a 7-year-old's brain isn't necessarily true for a 27-year-old's brain, so even a previously accurate diagnosis may no longer be the case for you.

And, even if it was accurate at the time, the label of that diagnosis does *not* have to stay with you for the rest of your life. Many successful survivors of childhood trauma have been labeled with Attention Deficit Disorder (ADD), Attention Deficit Hyperactive Disorder (ADHD), Oppositional Defiant Disorder (ODD), Attachment Disorder or Reactive Attachment Disorder (AD/RAD), Post-Traumatic Stress Disorder (PTSD), and myriad other diagnoses—sometimes with multiple diagnoses at once. But rather than accept those labels as life sentences, they focused on and leveraged their strengths and have turned their setbacks into successes. For example, say that the president of a large, extremely successful company exhibits attention deficit hyperactive traits. It obviously hasn't stopped him from being highly effective; in fact, because he never seems to slow down he probably gets more done in a week than many other people do in a month. The secret to his success is his having learned to very effectively channel all that nervous energy.

Oppositional defiance can also signify leadership qualities—precisely what is needed for an entrepreneur to succeed. People with attachment disorder tendencies tend to have one or two close friends rather than many casual friends. So what? Everyone, including the most well-adjusted people on earth, have their little quirks. Embrace your quirkiness and get on with your life, and refuse to use a mental health diagnosis as an excuse to limit your potential.

Begin to look dispassionately at your behavior following the difficult experiences in your life. These behaviors may no longer be appropriate to the life you lead now, or the life you wish to live. They may in fact be ongoing coping mechanisms, the ones you used to survive trauma, grief, and loss, and they may be outstaying their welcome. For example, if you bully or intimidate people to get what you want or need, rather than feeling guilty about it consider that your behavior may have been a means to survive that served you well—at a time in your life when you needed to appear stronger than you were. Make the determination to stop doing or saying things that could be considered threatening or intimidating. Those old behaviors no longer define you. Consider that those behaviors, along with the thoughts and comments that accompanied them, may be what led to your mental health diagnosis. Consequently, when you eliminate those thoughts, words, and behaviors, you may eliminate the diagnosis.

Coping mechanisms that served you for a time should be re-evaluated and either honed for use on the way to your good future or else discarded and left behind as a part of your past. For example, manipulation is a self-serving way of persuading people to do what you want them to do for *your* purposes, rather than for what's good for *them*. However, the core skill involved in manipulation is persuasion, which is a necessary tool for success in business. In fact, the Harvard Kennedy School says, "The capacity to persuade is key to effective leadership." They consider this skill so important, that they teach classes in the art of persuasion.

Persuasion is also the key to sales; someone who has learned to be a good manipulator to survive a dysfunctional childhood or abusive relationship can learn to use his or her skills of persuasion to help lead others to purchase a product or service that will be useful for them or that might even improve their lives exponentially. When a salesperson helps someone make a purchase that will help the buyer, both the salesperson and the buyer win. Real success happens when everyone involved benefits from the transaction.

If you are not sure which of your behaviors may have been coping mechanisms to help you get through rough times, read through the chapters of this book and think about where you see yourself. Each chapter goes into detail about the various skills that successful survivors use to survive trauma, and how they can be useful in the future. Another way to look at your behaviors more objectively is to ask a trusted friend or mentor what he or she sees. Be careful not to take offense at what you're told. Give the person permission to be honest, and ask for advice on how you can use those survival skills as positive tools for your future.

It should be said: some people truly are clinically depressed, and suffer from a chemical imbalance that must be regulated with medication. There's nothing wrong with working with a physician to find the dosage of medication and/or therapy that will assist in your fight against depression, or any other medical or mental health diagnosis. This is no different from diabetics taking insulin or hypertension patients taking medication to lower their blood pressure. What I'm suggesting here is not to *avoid* a medical approach; rather, do not rely solely on it. Successful survivors make proactive changes that get at the root cause of their feelings of sadness rather than relying solely on medication to do the work. After all, many medications can alleviate symptoms without "curing" the cause.

Treating your issues at their root is similar to diabetics changing their eating habits to eliminate foods with sugar, or people with hypertension exercising and eliminating excess salt from their diet. In other words, rather than sitting back and accepting depression—or any other mental or medical diagnosis—and allowing it to hold you back, take an honest, objective look at what you can do to improve your situation. Almost every situation can be improved by choosing to have a good attitude, choosing positive words and actions, exercising, getting more oxygen, drinking more water, eating fewer chemically laden or sugary foods, establishing a consistent routine of adequate sleep, and not putting harmful substances in your body.

That being said: if you *have* been prescribed medication to treat a mental health diagnosis, please do not arbitrarily quit your medication without first consulting your doctor. Measuring the chemicals in your brain isn't as accurate a science as measuring the sugar in your blood or calculating the pressure at which your heart is pumping blood. Treating mental issues is not yet an exact science, so if you try something that doesn't work well, don't just give up. Give it a fair amount of time, and know that your doctor may want you to try other medications and dosages a few times before dialing in the correct medication(s) for you.

If you find that your doctor doesn't have the time to work with you to find the right medication and dosage, find another doctor. If you do make changes to your diet, exercise, or medications, pay attention to your reaction and make a record of how you feel, along with any other pertinent data, so that you can share that information with your doctor.

Participate in an active way to track the results of therapy and medications. You are your own best advocate; you have the greatest vested interest in your well-being. You know your mind and body better than anyone else. So take charge and stick with it until you have the quality of life you want.

Many people point to a medical diagnosis of depression as though it were a "pass," so to speak, for their sadness. Rather than working to feel better and moving toward the fulfillment of goals that lead to a great life, some people prefer to use their diagnosis as an excuse to lower the expectations made of them. They are comfortable with the sympathy and pity that sometimes accompanies a diagnosis, so there's no incentive for them to change. People who haven't fought against depression may think the word *comfortable* is an odd choice of words, but those who have experienced depression know that it can feel like an old familiar blanket. Those who don't know how good it can feel to shed that cozy old blanket, or who fear they would feel guilty for moving on from the tragedy that led to curling up in it, will often intentionally surround themselves with the very things that trigger the memories that led to pain. They'll listen to the old music, look at the old pictures and read the old letters, finding an odd sort of comfort in their tears.

Successful survivors know that, although it can actually feel comforting to marinate in those negative memories, doing so takes us off course and sends us backward into the past, rather than forward into our future. When they feel that old familiar blanket dropping down on them, successful survivors intentionally listen to the music that gets them moving, smiling, and singing along. They watch television shows or movies that make them laugh, they reach out to help someone else, or remind themselves of past successes and future plans. Successful survivors figure out what gets them back on track, and they intentionally choose to do those things while avoiding anything that could drag them back into sadness.

People who are angry, unhappy, or depressed often indulge in self-destructive tendencies, such as smoking cigarettes, using drugs, eating to excess, and even driving recklessly. When depressed people drive while focused on their problems rather than the road ahead of them and the traffic around them, they are slower to react to another driver who is easing over into their lane than someone who believes he or she has a bright future to protect. Imagine the angry person who drives a little too fast on tires that can't handle a sharp turn. If the tire blows and an accident results, is it an accident? Bad luck? Or is it a form of indirect suicidal behavior? This may sound like an extreme notion, but Dr. Ellen Visser, a researcher at University Medical Hospital at Groningen, Netherlands, has asserted that failure to take care of one's vehicle, replace batteries in smoke detectors, visit the doctor for regular checkups, etc., are potentially indirect forms of suicide.[iii] Successful survivors avoid self-destructive tendencies; they take care of themselves and those around them.

Successful survivors choose to imagine a future with hope rather than one with more of the same pain. This choice to hang onto the hope that things can change, that we can participate in that change, and that things will not always be bleak is what allows us to step back from the edge and face our future head on. It's not that successful survivors haven't been to the edge; many have. But the difference between *acting* on destructive thoughts and *replacing* them with dreams of a better life is the four-letter word spelled **h-o-p-e**.

If you happen to be in the darkest time of your life as you're reading this, you may think that what I'm saying is nonsense. You may believe that depression has a hold on you and that you are powerless to do anything about it. In fact, you may be angry at the assertion that you can simply "pull yourself up by the bootstraps" and shed your depression. If so, consider that *hope* is one of the most powerful of human emotions. There are many compelling true stories of how hope kept people alive in the darkest of circumstances, from Nazi prison camp survivor Viktor

Frankl to the Chilean minors who were rescued after being trapped in a collapsed mine and presumed dead for 17 days.

You are not powerless. You have options. There is power inside of you that you haven't tapped yet. Determine right now to take suicide and self-harm off the table as an option. Suicide is a permanent solution to a temporary situation, and all situations are temporary. The one thing that is assured in this life is change. Dare to believe that the change in your future will be positive and not negative.

If positive thinking, optimism, and actively fighting depression are new concepts for you, read books and watch movies about others who successfully navigated the feelings of depression. Read about very accomplished people who fought depression like Winston Churchill, England's Prime Minister during WWII; Mike Wallace, newscaster and co-host of *60 Minutes*; and actress Brooke Shields, all of whom still worked and accomplished much while dealing with feelings of depression. Although it may seem difficult or even impossible for you to feel differently than you do now, you *can* do what so many other successful survivors have done before you. You can live through the depression *and* overcome it, just like you've lived through and overcome everything else, to reach the place you are now!

FIVE SUCCESSFUL SURVIVAL STRATEGIES:
Optimism and Positivity, and for
Resisting Depression

Create a chart that lists the date, what you did to support an optimistic perspective, and how you felt at the end of the day, on a scale of 1-10, 1 being lowest, 10 being totally positive and upbeat. For example, your chart could look like this:

Date	Positivity Supporting Activity	How I Feel
June 12	Got 7 1/2 hours sleep, walked for 22 minutes, drank 3 8-oz glasses of water	6.5
June 13	Got 5 hours sleep	4
June 14	Got 8 hours sleep, did 10 push-ups, 25 sit-ups, drank 5 8-oz glasses of water	8.5
June 15	Got 7 1/2 hours sleep, ran for 10 minutes, drank 4 8-oz glasses of water	8
June 16	Got 7 hours sleep, walked 10 minutes, drank 4 8-oz glasses of water, and went to my first 12-step meeting	7

Affirm yourself regularly by starting and maintaining your *Lifebook* (see Chapter 9). You can create your *Lifebook* in a journal, a large scrapbooking-type album, a three-ring binder, or electronically, on a computer or mobile electronic device. Figure out what works for you, and then set aside at least an hour every week to add to your *Lifebook*. On separate pages, write out your answers to each of the following questions: Who are you? What do you know for sure? What can you learn as you progress along your journey of life? What impact have the decisions you've made had on your life? What was the reasoning behind these decisions? What are your goals and aspirations?

Many people don't get the help they need because they don't know where to start. In each of the United States, we have government agencies set up to help people with just about every area of life. To find services near you, go online and search for the services you need. If you're not sure what you need, contact the nearest Department of Social Services and start there. They will be able to guide you toward other, specific services. Take advantage of the services you need. That's what they are there for.

If you have been diagnosed with an illness or condition, be determined to not let that define you. To help with seeing yourself as the awesome, whole person you are (rather than one particular diagnosis), make a list of all the qualities and characteristics that *do* define you. For example, your list might look like this:

My Characteristics	My Personality	My Talents	My Skills
I'm strong	I'm fun to be with	I'm good at math	I'm a good listener
I'm resourceful	I'm easy-going	I'm a good cook	I'm good at researching things on the internet
I'm optimistic	I like learning new things	I have a great sense of direction	I'm good at helping others resolve conflict by seeing each person's point of view

Carry around a small notebook or piece of paper with you every day for a month. Draw a "T" chart on the paper, with "Negative" at the top of the left side of the "T" and "Positive" on the top of the right side of the "T." Make note every time you catch yourself making a negative or a positive comment. Note the word you used, or just make a tick mark. Once you get used to catching those negative remarks, you'll be able to consciously choose to use more positive, optimistic words in your everyday conversations. This doesn't mean "sugar-coating" the truth, but rather reframing the truth into a more positive perspective. In some cases, some of the negative things that come out of our mouths simply do not need to be voiced at all. Your "T" chart may look like this:

Negative	Positive
Ugly	Potential for improvement
Stupid	Could use additional training
Idiot	May be making poor choices

SUMMARY

Many people are not naturally optimistic, and they can't imagine how to become that way. If you are one of these people, and you are not optimistic by nature, know that you can *become* optimistic by choice.

How?

By identifying and focusing on your strengths, and not wasting time worrying about your weaknesses. By reminding yourself of times when you've made it through other tough situations. By learning to love and be loved. By choosing to believe the best of others. By never giving another human the power to influence your life negatively. By reframing your circumstances to see feelings of depression as data telling you it's time to re-evaluate your strengths.

Rather than allowing feelings of depression to rule your present and future, do as psychiatrist Dr. Frederic Flach suggests: Eliminate the old notion that depression is a disease to be "treated," as though it were chronic or even terminal. Decide to view depression—which on the surface may look like a failure to cope—as evidence of resilience.

Develop a positive attitude by intentionally replacing negative thoughts with positive, hope-filled thoughts. Do this in much the same way as you change the channel on the television. When you notice a negative thought, intentionally change the channel of your mind to a positive thought. Develop positivity in your life by speaking only positive words, by taking responsibility for your attitude, words, and behaviors, and by not blaming others for your circumstances.

Depression can destroy positivity, optimism and, ultimately, your future. Although depression may be something you struggle with, you do not have to give in to it. You can choose to fight it. When you feel it coming on or experience a "known trigger," immediately take action. Refuse to give in to it in the same way that you refuse to give in to any other attack. Like someone who quits smoking but continues to want a cigarette, you may have to push through feelings of depression over and over again. For you, it may not be something that is done once and checked off the list forever. But if you force yourself to put one foot in front of the other and do what you know you must do, it *will* get easier and easier, and eventually it won't be a struggle at all.

Fight depression with your thoughts, words, and actions. Refuse to be defined by any mental health diagnosis. You are much more than any label can describe. Avoid all forms of self-destructive behavior. There is enough evil in the world that can potentially destroy us without us adding to it. Deliberately look for things to be grateful for in your life.

If optimism doesn't come naturally to you, it may feel awkward or disingenuous to act and speak in a way that isn't backed up by your feelings. But if you give this approach an honest try over a reasonable period of time, you will find your attitudes and demeanor beginning to line up with your words and actions. Regardless of whether or not you are naturally positive and optimistic, you can deliberately choose to incorporate those characteristics into your personality, thereby developing those traits.

The terms "keep your chin up" and "look on the bright side" aren't just trite, old expressions. They are real weapons to fight depression! Keeping your eyes up helps you avoid crying and helps refocus your mind from sadness to solutions, from what you don't have to what you do have—what you can be grateful for. Optimistic successful survivors have learned to focus on what good can come from their situations. They know that they have lived through difficult experiences before, and they expect to make it through the present as well.

KEY POINTS FOR DEVELOPING OPTIMISM, POSITIVITY, AND TO RESISTING DEPRESSION

- Try exercise, getting enough sleep, establishing a consistent routine, joining a 12-step program, or whatever works for you. Try various approaches and combinations of approaches, pay attention to how you feel, and stick with what works for you.
- Create your own *Lifebook* to remind yourself of past successes, times you felt unstoppable, times you were happy, things that made you laugh, plans for your future, and whatever else makes you feel good. Look at it the moment you begin to feel discouraged.
- If you need medical, psychological, or spiritual help, get the help you need. Don't be reluctant to see a doctor, psychologist, psychiatrist, a member of the clergy, or all of the above!
- Determine not to let a diagnosis or state of mind define you.
- Build hope by intentionally adopting optimistic words, expressions, and behaviors, and eventually your reality will line up with your efforts.

CHAPTER 4

Adaptability, Bravery, and Responsiveness

ADAPTABLE: flexible

BRAVE: bold; undaunted; fearless

RESPONSIVE: quick to react

CARISSA PHELPS, AUTHOR of *Runaway Girl*, was being prostituted by a brutal pimp by the time she was 12 years old. She had run away from home after learning that her stepfather was trying to sell her virginity to one of his buddies. One of 11 children, her mother didn't notice she was gone for several days. When Carissa finally managed to call for help, her mother dismissed her, saying, "You got yourself there, you can get yourself home."

Little Carissa was imprisoned for several years as a "reusable asset" of the trafficker and the woman who assisted him. They threatened to replace her with one of her younger sisters if she tried to run away, so to protect her sisters, she bravely stayed. To make it through the unspeakable horror of repeatedly being raped for money, Carissa somehow managed to adapt to her circumstances. This is not to say that she was okay with what was happening to her. But somehow, this young girl, alone and afraid, knowing that no one was looking for her, managed to bravely adapt to those who held her captive as she was bought and sold by many for several years. This is a level of bravery and adaptability on par with that of prisoners of war—perhaps even greater, given that POWs know that the power of their government is behind them, looking for them. No one was looking for Carissa.

The story of how Carissa Phelps went from being prostituted at 12 to graduating from UCLA with a law degree and an MBA, and becoming the founder and CEO of her company, Runaway Girl, is detailed both in her book and in the award winning documentary, *Carissa*. Her company, Runaway Girl, FCP, trains community leaders and law enforcement on understanding that under-aged youth who are being trafficked are not "prostitutes," but are rather victims of traffickers. She also trains them on appropriate care of human trafficking victims and encourages them to focus on prosecution of the real perpetrators: those who buy and sell children. Carissa and her Runaway Girl team aim to create employment and career development opportunities for former runaways and survivors of abuse, neglect, and trauma. It is a testament to her bravery, ability to adapt, and ability to respond to opportunities that Carissa has come through years of painful experiences to be the capable attorney, advocate, and businesswoman she is now.

The qualities of adaptability, bravery, and responsiveness can be summed up as "active coping." Coping with adversity refers to the ability to shift mindsets in the midst of crisis, turning from fear, which is passive, into action, to protect oneself and others and to prevent further harm. To adapt and bravely respond to ugly circumstances does not imply acceptance of those circumstances; rather, it is a survival skill which sets aside judgment of the situation for the time being and presses through, or else compartmentalizes, the feelings associated with what's happening.

As in the case of Carissa Phelps, many people find themselves in situations they are powerless to change. The ability to adapt and respond accordingly for a time is a valuable coping mechanism. People who have experienced childhood abandonment by a parent who was supposed to love and care for them are able to heal and move on from similar experiences more quickly than others who did not experience loss early in life. For example, a person whose father left the family and never returned has experienced a trauma that could be compared to losing a limb. It is gut-wrenchingly painful. But eventually, healing occurs. The one left behind realizes that life has, in fact, gone on. The planet has continued to turn, the sun continues to rise and fall in the sky. And in time, a new normal is developed. Enjoyment of life—an experience thought to have been lost forever—can begin to return.

When successful survivors go through this process of loss, grieving, and healing as young children, they learn earlier than most that they *can* survive. Then, when it comes to future loss—a best friend moves away, their significant other leaves them for someone else, or a loved one dies—they have the ability to heal and move past it more quickly than does the average person. Their experiences have taught them that the planet is still turning, despite what they're going through. They're still breathing—they're still in the game.

The ability of successful survivors to go through the process of trauma, loss, grief, and healing at a faster clip than most may seem abnormal to others. Because of what they've been through, some successful survivors may even take a sort of matter-of-fact approach to tragedy. It's not that it doesn't hurt; but having experienced such deep, raw pain before, some simply refuse to allow themselves to ever go there again. So they adapt to their new reality and respond by carrying on. Some would say they're "compartmentalizing" or suppressing their pain, and perhaps, for a time, they do. Or perhaps they avoid dealing with it entirely. So what? If they do so, they do so to survive. They pull themselves together and they go on, for themselves, for their families, and for the greater good.

Those who have learned how to survive in abusive or chaotic environments know how to quickly "throw the switch," changing from passive fear to active coping. This is the crux of responsiveness. Successful survivors of trauma and tragedy draw on the confidence gained through knowing they have made it through tough stuff before, and they will make it through whatever faces them in the future. Joel Osteen, best-selling author and senior pastor of Lakewood Church in Houston, said, "You don't know what's on the inside of you until you put a demand on your potential." Successful survivors have a better sense of what's hidden inside them, specifically *because* they've been put in situations that made demands on their potential.

Psychologists say that survivors of sudden and severe crisis survive because of their memories of having successfully survived before. The human brain is like a computer that, when faced with crises, searches for memories of similar situations. When the brain locks onto another time when the person survived, the brain goes into the same "survival mode" that worked in the past. It uses the critical thinking process that found a way out before.

On the other hand, people who have not experienced serious trauma have nothing in the memory banks of their minds with which to match the current situation. As a result, they may find themselves psychologically paralyzed, not knowing what to do. In an emergency situation, failure to act quickly can result in the loss of your life and the lives of those around you. For example, in the situation of a plane crash, if the person sitting next to the emergency exit door is screaming and wringing his hands rather than unlatching the door and throwing it out, that person could cause the death of himself and everyone else who is blocked from getting out that door.

To illustrate my point: when I was 9 years old, I was sitting on the front bench seat of our old car, between my grandfather, who was driving, and my grandmother. As we were driving in the slow lane of the freeway, my grandfather said that his arm was bothering him. Since he'd had two heart attacks previously, this got the attention of my grandmother and me. He didn't have a chance to pull off the freeway before he grabbed his chest and slumped over. He was unconscious, with his foot pressing on the gas pedal—on California's Interstate 10, between Ontario and San Bernardino.

Without stopping to give any thought to it, I reached over and took hold of the steering wheel while trying to hold his torso back with my elbow. With the other hand, I reached down and heaved his heavy leg up off the accelerator. I somehow got my left leg over his legs and stomped on the brake while steering the car over to the shoulder of the road.

After I turned the keys to stop the engine, I pulled the nitroglycerin pills out of his front shirt pocket and put one under his tongue. I climbed over my grandmother, who was crying and wringing her hands. It's unkind (but fairly accurate) to say that she was totally worthless in an emergency. I waited for a break in oncoming traffic and ran around to the driver's side to try to pull my grandfather out of the car. Someone stopped and helped me drag him out of the car and over to the shoulder where I administered CPR, just like the paramedics who responded to his last heart attack had taught me to do. Someone must have called the highway patrol because it didn't seem like very long before CHP officers and an ambulance showed up to take my grandfather to the emergency room of the nearest hospital. I was later told by the emergency room doctor that my prompt response to his symptoms likely saved his life.

Responsiveness is highly prized as part of any skill set. The U.S. military prepares soldiers to be responsive, to be brave, and to adapt during difficult circumstances. This process prepares the soldiers for combat and the living situations that accompany it. Police academies, fire science schools, and federal law enforcement agencies train in what is referred to as "discipline and mental toughness." Not unlike military training, law enforcement professionals are trained to quickly assess people and situations. They have to determine in a split second if a gun raised against them is a toy or a legitimate, imminent threat. And in that split second, they must act accordingly. They have to quickly assess if an assailant is someone who can be reasoned with or if the person is under the influence of a substance or is mentally ill. Again, all in a split second, they must act accordingly, or else they and those around them can die. On a regular basis, they are required to make snap judgments about whether or not a suspect is being truthful. And, as in many other scenarios, they have to be right—or their lives and those of others may be at risk.

As in the case of soldiers, law enforcement officers, and first responders, pilots are trained, both in flight simulations and in the air, to encounter every known possibility, including worst case scenarios, so that in the event of genuine crisis their training kicks in and they act almost automatically.

While learning the skills, strategies, and techniques that save lives, people who are able to shift quickly from fear to coping also learn to manage their fears and move *toward* a crisis, rather than run from it. They learn to assess the situation and the options quickly, and then act decisively. Similarly, successful survivors of trauma can shift into the coping mechanisms they learned before to successfully survive future crisis situations.

Training and experience operate like a vaccine. Hardship and pressure can build up immunity to future hardship and pressure. This holds true for victims of trauma and other kinds of adversity. Their experiences act like a boot camp of sorts (though for some, it was likely more like a combat zone, live ammunition and all) that has prepared them to handle almost anything. Rather than see themselves as victims, successful survivors look at themselves as having completed an ugly, no-holds-barred training course; and as graduates of this "course," they are prepared for whatever comes their way.

One illustration of the life-saving value of this kind of training is found in the life of Joe Peloso. On September 11, 2001, Joe was in charge of an insurance company office in Tower II of New York's World Trade Center. After the first plane hit and building security people told occupants to remain in their offices, Joe walked from desk to desk calmly telling his staff to join him and exit the building. His calm, yet serious demeanor led people to get off the phone, stop other conversations, put down their files, and follow Joe. As the second plane hit, Joe and his staff were already well on their way to ground level. And when the tower collapsed, they were out of the building and walking down the street to safety. As first responders charged toward the buildings, and the air filled with debris that made it difficult to breathe, Joe kept his cool and walked his people all the way out of New York and safely over into New Jersey. Every one of Joe's staff survived that day.

Joe doesn't tell this story. In fact, when asked about it, Joe downplays his role in the survival of his staff. But some of the people whom he escorted out of the building that day tell of Joe's military training showing through, as he took charge and sternly commanded that his coworkers leave immediately. Successful survivors exhibit bravery, they have an air of authority in crisis that is born out of a quick and confident response to the situation, and importantly, they have the resolute determination to survive.

Like Joe, most truly brave people don't describe themselves as such. They seem to have an inherent mix of confidence and humility that leaves them with no need to boast. The true reflection of bravery is moving directly forward without hesitation toward tough issues, challenges, and crises that others may shy away from, ignore, or avoid.

Homo sapiens have been adapting and changing to fit their environment for thousands of years. That's how our species has survived. Integral to adapting to people and situations is the ability to quickly assess the people and the environment around us. **When entering a new environment, successful survivors easily assess who is in charge, who has power, who is insincere, who is self-serving, what the echelon is, and**

how to position themselves for maximum leverage within the existing social structure. They are also often able to quickly assess threats, both to themselves and others—a skill that is necessary to the survival of law enforcement officers, security details, and soldiers in combat situations.

One such successful survivor, Jeremy Harvey, was in the child welfare system from the time he was 4 until he turned 23. During that time, he lived in many different places, ranging from residential care facilities to mental institutions, group homes, and foster homes, not to mention the time Jeremy spent homeless. To survive in all those different places, each with its own set of rules, guidelines, procedures, personalities, and cultures, Jeremy learned to adapt. Without the characteristic of adaptability, a move away from your school, friends, and everything you know can be traumatic. Imagine how it would feel to lose everything, or to have everything you know taken from you. Imagine it happening over and over again.

Remarkably, Jeremy was able to adapt to each new situation. He adapted to the different rules, the new people, and the various cultures. In so doing, he gained valuable experience in navigating different environments and family dynamics, learning to understand the motivations and agendas of different stakeholders. Ultimately, Jeremy learned what he had to do to thrive. He earned his Bachelor's degree in history and sociology, and went on to earn his postgraduate certificate in paralegal studies. Now, he is applying what he's learned to help foster kids in his role as the post-emancipation services specialist for the Office of the Public Guardian in Illinois. In this role, Jeremy is able to apply his own unique blend of empathy, an ability to identify resources, and communication skills to help foster kids identify and access resources, to better survive foster care and ultimately to thrive.

The ability to adapt allows successful survivors to conduct themselves properly, whether they are at home, staying with someone as a guest, in the workplace, at a construction site, in an elegant restaurant, or at an important meeting. Successful survivors have learned to blend in and act the part in any personal or business setting; they can interact comfortably with everyone from the cleaning crew to the governor.

FIVE SUCCESSFUL SURVIVAL STRATEGIES:
Adaptability, Bravery, and Responsiveness

Write out your life story as though you were a newspaper reporter, from a completely objective point of view. If you find you're being tempted to judge yourself in any way, flip that judgement on end; congratulate yourself for having done whatever you had to do to survive. If you hid, you weren't a coward—you were resourceful enough to find a place to hide. If you fought back, you were courageous enough to fight back, despite differences in size and strength. If you ran away, you were responsive enough to run. If you went along with things, you were clearly clever enough to do what had to be done in order for you to make it out alive. You are the one who gets to decide whether you see yourself as a victim or a successful survivor in the situations you've experienced. Quit criticizing and judging yourself—see yourself as the survivor you are.

Make a list of all the ways you have had to learn to adapt in order to: get along with others; keep your job; get a promotion; maintain a fragile relationship, etc. You may not even be aware of (or given yourself credit for) all the times you've had to adapt to people and situations. Think back on the challenges, problems, and irritants you've had to deal with, and include them on your list. Examples of adapting can be as simple as learning to work with a difficult boss or co-worker, or learning how to avoid confrontation by changing your routine (for example, taking a different lunch time from a difficult person), or as complicated as learning sign language to be able to communicate with someone who is deaf. You've had to adapt to different places you've lived, different styles of leadership of the people with authority over you, and myriad other challenges. Give yourself credit for the extremely valuable skill of being to adapt to various circumstances.

Write down the times you've been brave. Don't worry about whether anyone else would consider you brave in the circumstance. This is for you—no one else. Don't skip this step. Exhibiting bravery can include facing a phobia—for example, someone who struggles with claustrophobia getting into an elevator and allowing the doors to close with them inside. It can mean someone who is afraid of the dark sleeping with the light off. It can be someone fearful of high places going to the top floor of a high-rise building. It can even mean what people often think of when they hear the word, "bravery": firefighters going into a burning building, soldiers being deployed into a combat zone, or police officers responding to a "shots fired" call.

Go through the list of the times you've adapted and the times you've exhibited bravery. Note which times your response contributed to your getting through the difficult situation. Did you quickly call for help? Did you say, "No!" to an aggressor or to a demanding person? Did you busy yourself with something else to get your mind off of a seemingly no-win situation? Did you get away quickly enough to avoid worsening of the situation? Don't diminish the value of your responses. Give yourself credit for doing the best you knew how to do under difficult circumstances. Whatever you did is evidence of your ability to cope and your style of coping.

As you review what you've written—your story, your bravery, your adaptations, and your responsiveness—give yourself credit for successfully surviving the challenges you faced. Don't blame yourself for doing less than you feel you should have. Say *no* to guilt! Refuse to feel guilty for not doing any more, or for not doing something different than you did. Do not compare yourself with anyone else; do not allow others to compare your responses to anyone else's. People are quick to say what *they* would have done in a certain set of circumstances, but the truth is that no one can say exactly what he or she would have done in the same situation. Others have overcome their own challenges, but none of us has ever truly walked in another person's shoes. If this particular issue is a stumbling block on the path toward your successful life, write out, "*I did the best I could do under the circumstances. I cannot go back in time and change even the slightest detail of what happened. But I can reframe my recollection of it to give myself credit for surviving the ordeal. And in doing that, I will go from survivor to successful survivor.*" Write it out as many times as it takes to get that truth into your head, and for it to drop the 18 inches from your head to your heart. Get it so deeply inside you that you will *never* forget it!

SUMMARY

You may have never thought about it, but if you've experienced trauma, you have the skills you need to navigate successfully through a crisis. You can utilize mental toughness and resist the urge to panic. In fact, you can shut *off* the panic button, instead tapping into your deepest strengths, your natural abilities and the coping mechanisms developed through other difficult circumstances that you have experienced. You may be screaming on the inside, but on the outside, you retain the ability to adapt to the situation and remain calm enough to do whatever you need to do to survive.

You have the ability to exhibit bravery in response to a crisis, while others around you fall apart or are immobilized with fear. You may have never given yourself credit for it, but you are likely able to channel your fear into determination to survive. And, after you've survived, your mind automatically files away the details of the tragedy for future reference. In other words, successful survivors don't dwell on what they have been through. Instead, they mine the lessons out of what they've been through, give themselves credit for the coping mechanisms and survival skills that helped them survive, and focus on their future.

In the event of an emergency, be the successful survivor (or else seek out the successful survivor, and do what they do). If you do that, your chances of survival will improve exponentially!

KEY POINTS FOR DEVELOPING ADAPTABILITY, BRAVERY, AND RESPONSIVENESS

- Take a fresh look at what you've experienced in your life and give yourself credit for surviving. When you see yourself as a survivor rather than a victim, it's easier to see the powerful, yet often subtle, characteristics that make you a successful survivor.

- When you have adapted to different people, different rules, cultures, styles of humor, or whatever else you've learned to adapt to, understand that you have mastered a highly valuable, transferrable skill.

- Consider times that you have faced a crisis, challenge, or anything that pushed you out of your comfort zone. Some way, somehow, you've survived, you've coped; you have been brave. When necessary, you can intentionally use your bravery again.

- When you have responded to difficulties without panicking, know that you can do it again. In fact, every time you respond to something that's difficult, you improve your ability to do so. It's like building a muscle! Rather than dismissing your past responsiveness, give yourself credit for getting up out of bed and moving forward, especially when you don't feel like it.

- Don't make the mistake of comparing the way you handled situations in your past with the ways others have or with the ways characters in film have. Too many people diminish or dismiss their coping mechanisms and good characteristics entirely, simply because they didn't handle a situation as cleverly as James Bond or Jason Bourne. Don't confuse fantasy with real-life situations; you're reading this, so you've survived, and you're well on your way to being a real-life successful survivor!

CHAPTER 5

Resiliency

RESILIENT: recovering and coming back stronger
after being knocked down; re-creating oneself time and again

O NE DAY, WHEN Adam Robe was five years old, he came home from kindergarten only to have his mother take him and his two siblings to the bus station, pin a note to his brother's shirt, and put them on a bus to live with his grandparents. She had purchased a one-way bus ticket to a different state hundreds of miles away. With no food, water, or money, little Adam rode that bus for hours with no idea why Mommy suddenly sent him away. When the bus finally arrived at its destination, he got off the bus, wandered around scared, cold, hungry, and stunned by this sudden upheaval of everything he had ever known. While wandering around in this unfamiliar place, 5-year-old Adam was finally picked up by the police. After his grandparents refused to take him and his siblings in, they were placed in foster care as they could not locate his mother. That was many years ago. In an effort to learn more about his childhood, Adam did locate and meet his mother 37 years after she abandoned him.

Adam Robe is one of the most resilient people I've ever known. He has used his resilience, along with his other skills, talents, abilities, and education, to help children who suffer through trauma, loss, and grief. If you met Adam Robe, MSW, author of the *Robbie the Rabbit* series of therapeutic children's books, you would have no idea that this intelligent, articulate, and thoughtful man had endured such painful abandonment. Adam's series of children's books help kids cope with the pain of abandonment, abuse, and other mistreatment that Adam knows intimately. Adam is happily married with a beautiful family. He is a spokesperson for the estimated 12 million alumni of the foster care system and is a practicing social worker. His experiences as a young child have equipped him to help children as well as his foster alumni "brothers and sisters."

Successful survivors have been knocked down—some literally, others figuratively. But when they get knocked down, they refuse to *stay* down. Successful survivors know that they got back up before, so when they are down, they immediately begin looking for ways to get back up again. Very often, they get back up stronger than ever before.

Of course, being resilient doesn't mean that you never face any difficulties or challenges. In fact, the very definition of being resilient implies that you face difficulties and successfully overcome them. The key to being resilient is the way you look at the challenge. You can look at difficulty as an insurmountable excuse for declaring failure, or you can make the choice to look at it as a challenge to overcome and an opportunity to grow.

Resilient people look at painful events like they would an inoculation. An inoculation works by injecting your body with the very infection you wish to ward off, so that pinpointed antibodies are built up. These antibodies make the person less susceptible to the infection if and when they are exposed to it in the future. Resilient people look at the painful events of their past as things that have influenced their minds, their will and their emotions, to help them deal effectively with future, potentially painful situations.

Because of the "inoculation" they've experienced, the resiliency they develop helps successful survivors respond to hurt differently than others would. For example, a person with a "victim mentality" might say, "I knew it was only a matter of time before you would hurt me. Everyone eventually does." Resilient people decide ahead of time not to give anyone the power to do them serious harm. They determine ahead of time not to be in a serious relationship with harmful or toxic people. They decide not to take offense at the words or actions of well-intentioned people, even when those otherwise good people are acting like knuckleheads. Resilient people don't allow themselves to be abused; neither do they allow themselves to become hyper-sensitive. Resilient people have lived through crisis before, so they know that the present troubles are temporary, and with time will pass.

Little Sophie Janczur was 11 years old when the Russian soldiers pounded on her door in the middle of the night. It was 1939, and Sophie knew that there was a war going on somewhere far away, but she was insulated from it. Sophie and her 3-year-old brother had been born into a well-to-do family. Sophie loved and was loved by her parents, was cared for by a nanny whom she adored, attended private school, and was driven around by a chauffeur in a Buick that had come all the way from America. So, you can imagine the shock little Sophie felt as she watched the Russian soldiers roust her mother and father out of bed and take them into custody for immediate "deportation." Sophie heard one of the soldiers whisper to her, "Get your coat and boots." Without a word, she went to fetch a coat and boots for herself and her little brother. She later realized that this was a rare kindness shown by one of the soldiers responsible for changing the lives of Sophie and her family forever.

Sophie never returned home again. She never saw her beloved spaniel, Drops, again. Sophie never learned what became of her dog, her home, or her family's belongings. The family was taken to the train station and loaded, along with many other families that had been taken into custody that night, into a train car that had been used to haul coal. When the train car couldn't hold a single additional person, the train left the station. People were standing pressed next to one another in the filthy coal car. As the train began to roll down the tracks, the coal dust from the roof began to drop on everyone. Before long, they were all covered with coal dust. It was difficult to breathe. There was no bathroom—only a hole in the middle of the train car floor.

For two excruciatingly long weeks, Sophie, her family and all the others on the train existed on the meager portions of cabbage soup and water given to them when the train stopped each day. The train finally came to the end of the tracks at a camp in Siberia. The families lived and worked at the "settlement camp" for about a year, existing on little more than small portions of turnips and potatoes and a 50-pound bag of rice that Sophie's father had traded for a 4.5-carat flawless diamond he had cleverly hidden in his shoe the night the family was arrested.

When the United States joined the war in December 1941, Sophie, her family, and all the families that had been "deported" to Siberia were released. The problem was that all of the people who were released had no place to go. All their homes had been confiscated by the communist government of what was then the Soviet Union. Despite having no place to go, Sophie's parents knew they had to get out of Siberia, but there was no way out—except for the train. They had no money, but Sophie still had her little girl's watch that she'd been wearing when she was taken into custody. It no longer worked, but it was pretty, so the train conductor let them get on the outbound train in exchange for the only thing Sophie had left from her former life—her watch.

For the next three years, Sophie and her family made their way out of Siberia, through Europe to Iran, and they eventually settled in England. Along the way, many people, including Sophie's father, died of starvation or from the extreme cold or from physical illness. Sophie had grown up quickly in the harsh circumstances of the impoverished camp and the subsequent travel. After settling in England, she met and married a young Polish man. They moved to the United States in search of the American dream. They built a life and a family in southern California.

Sophie has said that, somewhere in that first couple of weeks of riding in that coal train, dirty, hungry, and frightened for the first time in her life, she made the decision that she was going to make it. "It was as if a survival gene kicked in," Sophie said. She attributes her survival and the happy life that followed to three things: the love her family had for one another, adopting a positive attitude despite what was happening, and a sense of humor. The "survival gene" Sophie referred to is resilience.

When asked what characteristics all those experiences had built in her, Sophie responded enthusiastically and with a big smile that she has learned to "appreciate everything." She refuses to judge or criticize anyone. She understands that many of the difficult circumstances people face are completely out of their control. Sophie doesn't exhibit even the slightest hint of self-pity. Rather, she has a bright smile and a beautiful attitude of gratitude for the good life she has.

Like Sophie, when you shift from the mindset of being overwhelmed by a challenge into making the decision to survive it, you begin to look for the opportunities in the challenge. Your brain automatically begins to look for ways to survive. Your brain can operate more efficiently than any computer when the right questions are posed. For example, consider what your brain does with this statement: "*What's happened is awful. Why did this happen?! What's going to happen to me now? I didn't sign up for this. I'm not prepared for this. Oh, no!*" Your brain is now processing an awful event that appears to be outside of your control. Now, imagine your brain processing the following: "*What's happened is awful. What can I do to get through this? How might I bring good from this? How can I use this situation to my advantage? How can I come back stronger?*" The computer that is your brain will automatically get to work and come up with various solutions to the questions posed. Not all solutions may be viable, and the timing might not be right for others. The point is to get your brain calculating possible solutions rather than circling around in a loop over the present circumstances.

Another way that your brain can work to find the solutions you need to the challenges you face is to use your ability to imagine a future where the "resilient you" has triumphed over your current challenges. Everything you use today was once the subject of someone's vivid imagination. Many inventions were the result of the use of the inventor's imagination being used to find solutions to the problem he or she faced. If you've survived trauma, you've likely used your imagination in ways that you haven't yet realized. Many of us developed vivid imaginations to mentally escape what was happening to us or what was going on around us when our situations became overwhelming. Some of us had our imaginations and dreams squelched by others. By reconnecting with your ability to imagine better scenarios, you can work to develop resiliency and to solve problems in your life.

One practical way to do this is to get pen and paper, and begin to write down possible solutions. Do not dismiss anything; write down even the most seemingly absurd ideas. Later, sit down and sort through them, assessing their viability. The more possible solutions you come up with, the better you'll feel. You'll begin to think that you actually *can* do something to affect change in your situation. But the first step is to get your brain working on those possible solutions. Once you begin to implement this technique, you'll find that every time you use it you'll come up with more potential courses of action.

Once you've made your list of options, assign a priority to each possible solution, starting with the most easily implementable, down to the ones that are a real long shot. Next, systematically go down the list, imagining how you might implement each of these possible solutions. In this process, you may discover additional information that causes you to revise an idea or else re-evaluate the priority of ideas. The point here is that resilient people *will* find a way to bounce back!

One example of clever and resilient people finding their way to bounce back is a pair of brothers who together owned a telemarketing firm. They sold their service of "cold calling" potential business prospects to insurance agencies who wanted to outsource this difficult and often unpleasant job. However, when a law was passed that allowed people to place their telephone numbers on a "do not call" list, the number of potential clients who could be reached by phone was significantly decreased, and this lucrative business dried up almost overnight.

As their clients canceled contracts, the brothers had no choice but to lay off employees. There wasn't enough income coming in to pay the owners or even to pay the basic expenses. The business was failing, the brothers were getting behind in their personal bills, and their families were worried. But rather than get discouraged, angry, depressed, or else numbing their disappointment with alcohol or drugs, the two brothers began to inventory their skills, talents, abilities, and business relationships. They talked to the various business people with whom they had worked and asked about their needs. They then strategized about how they might match their skills, talents and abilities with the other needs of their clients. From their strategy session and client meetings was born a business that is now bigger, more profitable, and more efficient than the one they had before!

While many people view the kinds of problems faced by those two brothers as impossible to overcome, those men saw their adversity as a challenge that they could turn into an opportunity. They worked hard at reinventing themselves, an effort that has paid off for them in ways they couldn't have even imagined before. The best news is that they are now helping people in ways they had not foreseen. Their new business matches insurance brokers with insurance companies that specialize in protecting specific types of businesses. For example, when insurance brokers find themselves faced with properly insuring a type of business with which they have no experience, they can go to the website of the brothers' "new and improved" business and search for the keywords of the industry that the broker is trying to insure. The website lists the various insurance companies that specialize in insuring that type of business, making it quick and easy to find the right insurance company and coverage for even the most obscure types of businesses. As a result, brokers spend less time trying to find the right insurance companies, and the client winds up with better coverage and premiums with an insurance company that understands their particular risks. Everyone wins!

It's significant to point out that the brothers had no prior experience in creating Internet-based programs or doing Internet marketing; they hired the expertise they needed. Their ingenuity came in asking their clients what they needed, and in attempting to find a solution to the challenges their clients mentioned. Notice that they didn't try to change the law that had essentially put them out of business. Neither did they close up shop and go home, bemoaning the unfairness of the hand they'd been dealt. Their ultimate success came from a resilient attitude that drove them to push through the seemingly insurmountable challenges before them, only to come out better and stronger than ever before.

During my 20 years as an employer, I went through several challenges that could have put me out of business entirely. A partner stole $38,000 from me; an employee stole a credit card and used it to charge up thousands of dollars for a new wardrobe and furnishings for the office she was setting up to compete with me; and I lost my primary insurance company partner, to name just a few.

The insurance company that I had partnered with had been in business since the mid-1700s and had an excellent financial rating, when the unthinkable happened: they went bankrupt. This was a devastating blow to me, as one by one my clients had no choice but to move their insurance to my competition. I was devastated as I watched my business, which I built through years of working 80–100 hour weeks, fall apart virtually overnight.

I could have chosen to go out of business and work for someone else, where I wouldn't have to deal with these kinds of pressures. In fact, others in similar positions *did* close their doors. One of those people who lost his business suffered a nervous breakdown; another man, whose business depended on that insurance company, tragically committed suicide. My reaction to the challenge of losing my insurance company partner was instead to obtain a list of all the insurance companies in the United States, and to begin to call the CEOs of those companies, asking them if they would be willing to insure homes for abused children—the type of organization my company was founded to protect. At that time, these homes were not the desired target class of business for any insurance companies in the United States.

In most cases my phone calls weren't successful, but I wasn't discouraged. I knew from my time as a 15-year-old telemarketer that eventually someone would hear me out! And in fact, someone *did*: Tom Mulligan, now retired president of Western World Insurance Company, agreed to listen to my proposal. That first conversation led to both a working relationship, which lasted until I sold my company many years later, and a friendship that continues to this day.

To endure these and other business crises over the years, I used the resiliency skills I learned by surviving and coping with the abandonment, neglect, abuse, and poverty of my childhood. They turned out to be exactly the skills I needed to bounce back from everything that threatened the survival of my business. With each adversity I faced in business, I knew that no person and no business had the power to hurt me as badly as I had been hurt as a child. I knew that somehow, some way, I would recover from even the most devastating situations and come back stronger after being knocked down.

This characteristic of resiliency can save your life. To illustrate this fact, consider the person facing a diagnosis of cancer. Although the mention of the word *cancer* elicits fear in everyone, the resilient person shifts into survival mode. He or she begins to learn about the particular strain of disease attacking his or her body, investigates various treatments, seeks out specialists, consults with others, and actively cooperates with a plan to regain wellness. Resilient people shift into survival mode because they know how to do so; they've done it before, so it's natural, in some cases even automatic.

A person with little resilience asks, "How long do I have to live?" and then proceeds to prepare for the end. It is natural to ask this question, and I don't mean to imply that the person asking it is somehow wrong to do so. What I *am* saying is that asking this question points our mind toward the *problem*, rather than the *solution*; it puts our survival in the hands of someone else, because it introduces the suggestion that the end of our life is imminent.

Regardless of the challenges you face in your life, make the determination to refuse anyone the power to direct your life. Don't give anyone, including well-meaning medical professionals, the opportunity to give you a death sentence. The naked truth is that we are all dying; no one escapes this life without experiencing death. The question is not, "Will I die?" Of course you will. Neither is the question, "*When* will I die?" No one really knows that. Many people have been given a death sentence and proceeded to live many years beyond anyone's expectations. **The question for resilient people is, "What can I do that is of the highest significance between now and the day I die—regardless of how long that is?"**

Resilient people take responsibility for their survival, their quality of life, their peace, and their ability to thrive. They may step back, assess their situation, and create a new goal, but they refuse to consider anything other than their desired result. Consequently, resilient people have a much better chance of rebuilding their business, outliving a negative prognosis, or beating the odds in any challenge, all while having peace of mind in the midst of crisis.

FIVE SUCCESSFUL SURVIVAL STRATEGIES:
Resilience

Put together a list of the specific challenges you've faced. List the valuable skills and lessons you've learned, and the characteristics you've developed as you lived through those challenges (we'll talk more about this important step in Chapter 9). For now, understand that the characteristic of resilience is essentially the lifelong process of learning to apply the skills, lessons, and characteristics acquired in adversity. As you face the inevitable ups and downs of life, you should strive to make use of similar experiences in your past to better meet these challenges. And every time you use a skill, it becomes easier for you to use it in the future. Think of developing resiliency like learning to ride a bicycle. When you're first learning, you're focused on trying to balance, pedal, use the brakes, not crash into something, and not fall off the bike. But the more you ride, the better you get, until riding the bike comes almost as naturally as walking. The more you intentionally use what you've learned and acquired in adversity, the stronger your resilience will become.

In a personal journal, write down five things you're grateful for at the start of every day. If you can't think of anything, consider the fact that you just by reading this, you've taken the first step toward becoming your ideal you—a first step that many struggle to take. Forcing yourself to think of five things for which you are grateful turns your attention from what you lack to what you have. Your brain kicks into gear, looking for things to be grateful for, rather than complaining about what you don't have or what others aren't doing for you. At the end of each day, do the same thing. Write down five things that happened (or disasters that didn't happen) for which you are grateful. This serves to focus your mind on positive things right before you drift off the sleep. This one activity can transform your attitude and help to build your resilience.

If there is a television show or movie that makes you laugh, watch it when you feel yourself slipping into sadness or frustration. Laughter relieves tension and gives you a respite from the troubles you face. It's a healthy alternative to alcohol, drugs, or any of the other distractions that people use to take their mind off their problems.

Every morning, ask yourself, *"How can I improve my life today?"* Write out your answer. This engages your brain in the work of finding solutions, rather than hitting the wall trying to answer questions like, *"Why is my life this way?"* Consider asking yourself how you can use your considerable skills, talents, abilities, and characteristics to help others. This one question can lead to breakthroughs in your personal and professional life that you may not have dreamed possible.

Most people spend more time making plans for the weekend than they do making plans for their lives! Schedule time alone when you can devote yourself to considering specifically what *you* want for your future. With each thing you would like to have or do, answer the question, *"How can I make this a reality in my life? What five things can I do in the next week to move closer to the attainment of these goals?"*

SUMMARY

You are probably more resilient than you give yourself credit for. And even if you aren't, the good news is that you can develop the characteristic of resiliency by making the decision now to keep on trying after every disappointment and setback. Consider the resilience of other successful survivors, who got up after being knocked down time and again. Determine for yourself to get back up, regardless of how many times it takes.

As Dr. Frederic Flach says in his book *Resilience*: "…the [ongoing] regulation of self-esteem is what counts, not a fixed state of self-satisfaction or discontent." By giving yourself credit for the characteristics you've developed in adversity, as well as for your natural talents, abilities, and learned skills, you'll be helping yourself to regulate your self-esteem, which will in turn help you to maintain the resilience needed for bouncing back from whatever challenges you face. In fact, understanding your unique combination of "successful survivor skills" and other personal assets can help you not *only* to bounce back, but lunge *forward* toward the establishment of your personal and professional success.

Think of all you've successfully lived through so far. Don't focus on what you did wrong or what you may have failed to do; focus on the fact that you have made it through some tough times. You're still alive! And you have skills, talents, and abilities that you may not have even tapped yet. There is still a good plan to be had for your life; it's up to you to find and fulfill it.

Ask yourself how you survived the challenges you've faced in the past. Mine the lessons out of those experiences. Did those tough times build patience? Empathy? A desire for justice? Did you learn to adapt to different people and circumstances? How did you cope? Did you learn to read facial expressions, body language and other clues from the people involved? Did you learn how to take care of yourself? Did you learn how to comfort others? Did you use your imagination to envision a brighter future?

Resilient people are the ones who create their own success by analyzing what went wrong before and come up with a different approach for tomorrow. They're the ones who, no matter what, know to hang onto hope and refuse to give up!

KEY POINTS FOR DEVELOPING RESILIENCE

- View the painful events and challenges of your life as an inoculation against future challenges. Once you learn that resilience is an on-going regulation of self-esteem, you can begin to intentionally use this new-found characteristic to ride out the roller coaster of life.

- Adopt an attitude of gratitude for everything you *do* have rather than focusing on what you *don't* have.
- Intentionally use your sense of humor. Watch a funny movie, subscribe to a daily joke list, or read a funny book. Find someone who has a good attitude, punctuated by a healthy sense of humor, and spend time with him or her.
- Put your brain to work by asking the right questions. Rather than asking "why" questions, ask "how" questions. How can I improve this situation? What can I do right now to move toward the outcome I would like to see?
- Consider the other people who have come back stronger after very difficult setbacks—Steve Jobs being fired from Apple, Oprah Winfrey fired as a TV news anchor, Walt Disney filing for bankruptcy. These and many more gained their greatest successes after what appeared to be their biggest setbacks!

CHAPTER 6

Courage

COURAGE: the quality of mind or spirit that enables a person
to face difficulty, danger, pain, etc., without fear; bravery

---

IT TOOK COURAGE for the very skinny, very young, and very white pastor to walk through the rough streets of Los Angeles at 2 AM. He was unaccustomed to chatting with people who were drunk or high, or those who were selling drugs (or themselves). His white skin and blond hair must have been as visible as a lit-up glow stick as he walked through that dangerous neighborhood. But that single act of courage would change his life—and the lives of countless others.

Matthew Barnett's dream was to build a church in Los Angeles, similar to what his father, Pastor Tommy Barnett, had done in Phoenix with the First Assembly of God Church. But rather than see his congregation grow and thrive, the 39 people Pastor Matthew ministered to every Sunday eventually dwindled down to zero. One night, the anguished young pastor prayed, cried, tossed, and turned, but couldn't rest. So he got up and started walking around the very dangerous neighborhood where he rented a small apartment.

He described what he saw as "one giant urban crime scene." He saw three police cars with lights ablaze and five armed police officers with two young men handcuffed, leaning spread-eagle against the wall. There was a group of people drunk on the front porch of a nearby house. Two people were squaring off to fight one another. A helicopter flew overhead, its powerful searchlight trained on a spot nearby in search of a fleeing suspect. There were homeless people with shopping carts, drug deals going down in the shadows, and a pregnant teenager looking frightened and alone. The young, clean-cut pastor (raised in an upper class area of Phoenix) had never seen anything like what he witnessed that night. As he stood on the street watching what transpired there every night of the week, he knew that he hadn't been brought to Los Angeles to build a church; rather, he had been called to help build *people*.

The result of that one night was what is now known as The Dream Center, commonly referred to as "the church that never sleeps." The Dream Center is part homeless shelter, part mobile food program, part transitional living home for young adults who have aged out of the foster care system. It provides residential care for rescued trafficking victims, serves as a mobile medical clinic, a soup kitchen, a sober living program, and so much more. At the time of this writing, The Dream Center serves more than 30,000 people every single week.

And none of that would have happened if that skinny young pastor hadn't had the courage to walk through the gang- and drug-infested streets that night.

Pastor Matthew Barnett's courage has fueled a transformation in the lives of the thousands of people who have been loved into wholeness at the Dream Center. And there are now Dream Centers popping up all over the country, helping countless others—all because of the courage of one young man from Phoenix. Pastor Matthew found his cause lay at the intersection of the needs of others and what he could do to try to meet those needs. The stories of some of the amazing transformations worked by The Dream Center can be found in his book, *The Cause within You: Finding the One Great Thing God Created You to Do in This World.*

There are few examples of courage more profound than one child protecting a younger sibling by offering him- or herself up to an abuser. And sadly, this happens all too often. This kind of courage is illustrated in the story of a friend (who prefers to remain anonymous, for reasons that will be obvious shortly), whom we'll call Maria. Maria was left in an orphanage in Mexico for many years with her younger sister and brother while their mother went to the United States to find work, in the hopes of returning for them someday. The man and woman who ran the orphanage sexually molested Maria from the time she was 6 years old. Because she didn't want the same thing to happen to her sister, she would put her little sister in bed first, so that her sister was against the wall. She would then take the outside position; at just 6 years of age, she was always thinking of ways that she could distract the abuser from her sister when he came in the room after everyone had gone to bed. She would also offer to go with him so that he wouldn't hurt her sister. The boys slept in a different building, so she couldn't protect her brother. Years later, she learned that her brother, equally defenseless, was being molested as well. To this day, she carries unwarranted guilt about not being able to protect her brother.

Imagine the courage it took for that little girl to experience the pain and shame that accompanies years of sexual abuse, all in an effort to keep her little sister safe. Years went by without any word from their mother. At first Maria held onto the hope of being saved from the situation, but eventually she came to terms with the understanding that her mother wasn't coming back, and that there was no one who was going to rescue her and her siblings. Nearly eight years later, after the children had lost hope of ever seeing their mother again, Maria's mother finally returned to take her children out of the orphanage and into their new life in the United States.

Neither Maria nor her siblings ever told their mother what happened to them at the orphanage. To this day, their mother thinks that the nice couple who ran the orphanage were good people, who cared for children out of the kindness of their hearts. Maria prefers to keep her secret, knowing that the truth would hurt her mother, and that no good can come from telling her now—it will not change the past.

Maria has been happily married to a good man for many years, and they have two wonderful children. The courage she showed as a little girl has continued to help her through many trying times in her adult life. It took courage for Maria to forgive her mother for leaving her and her siblings behind. It took courage to learn to trust the man who became her husband. And it took courage for her to tell her story—a story she'd never told anyone other than her husband. Maria has put the past where it belongs—behind her. It has no place in the good life she lives now. She has left it in the past, where it can no longer hurt her.

When asked what advice she would give to anyone who has gone through something like she endured, without hesitation Maria said, "Forgive the people who mistreated you and those who allowed the abuse to happen. Don't take it out on people who had nothing to do with the abuse. Don't think about what happened. Don't complain about what happened. Focus your life and your energy on your present and your future." Good advice, from a courageous, successful survivor of years of abuse.

Successful survivors are courageous enough to believe there is something better in their future. When there's little reason to hope for improvement, it takes courage to continue to hang onto whatever small glimmer of hope may remain. There may be occasional feelings of helplessness or hopelessness, but the courageous successful survivor always manages to draw on their inherent fortitude to channel the fighting spirit that has served them well in past adversities.

By fighting spirit, I don't mean to suggest that successful survivors are obstinate or antagonistic. Rather, fighting spirit means a refusal to give up, to give in. They won't accept the diagnosis of a death sentence without a fight. They won't cower or back down from defending themselves, and they will often step up to defend someone else who is vulnerable. Successful survivors often find themselves in careers that seek justice for others, such as law enforcement, probation, and the military. They make good lawyers, court-appointed special advocates, missionaries, and many other positions that involve advocating for those who aren't able to stand up for themselves.

People who have been through some really difficult circumstances, especially when they were powerless to avoid it or prevent it, are often more courageous than the average person. I'm not talking about "acting tough," although that *can* be an indicator of courage. **Often, courage shows up in the form of quiet resolution.** Truly courageous people often remain quiet and in the background. But when they are called upon, they step up, accomplishing tasks that would overwhelm most people.

One example of courage as quiet resolution is found in the life of a high school senior whom we'll call Leyla. We're not using her name here because, at the time of this writing, she is a minor who for the first time recently revealed the physical, emotional, and sexual abuse she has lived with for the past eight years. For almost half of her life, she has been demeaned, beaten, and humiliated at home. Yet at school, Leyla is a popular, friendly cheerleader who maintains an excellent grade point average. Not a single person in Leyla's life has ever suspected that she had anything other than a great family and home life. Now that Leyla has shared her secret, the tectonic shifts that she and her family will go through in the coming months and years are likely to be very difficult. But the courage and quiet resolution that it took to live through the horror of her home life and still put on a performance at school worthy of an Academy Award will carry her through what's next, as well as through any other difficulties she faces in her future.

Many successful survivors show courage by trying to protect others from physical abuse. In my case, when my grandfather got violent, he would lash out at whoever was closest to him. And in the tiny, garage-size shack we lived in, there was nowhere to go to get away from him. In just a few steps, he could cover the entire little shack. Even though my grandmother was abusive toward me as well, I saw her as a victim, and was therefore very protective of her. She was 5 feet 7 inches and weighed barely over 100 pounds—she was no match for my grandfather, who was taller, bulkier, and stronger. He could overpower her with one punch, and when he would grab her and throw her against the wall, I would fly between them, a half-inch from his face as he was screaming and spitting.

Some of my grandfather's wild blows connected with me, but I could never walk away and leave him to pound on my grandmother. She would slide down the wall and cower on the floor behind me. Although I was just a little girl, I would stand right up to him and stare him square in the eyes. In hindsight, I can see myself standing there, absorbing the verbal abuse like a barrier that covered and protected my grandmother. When I took blows, I did all I could to avoid crying, and I never begged for him to stop. I'd stand as tall as I could, squinting my eyes while staring directly into his. I wanted him to see that he couldn't break me.

When my grandfather would regain some control of his senses, he would tell me that he would stop the punishment if I would cry or say I was sorry—for what, I still have no idea. But back then, I was too stubborn to say that I was sorry for some mysterious wrong I knew nothing of, or for something I had not done. So, while the beatings were probably prolonged by my actions, I can't go back and change any of it now. What I *can* do is to look dispassionately at the situation and give myself credit for having had the courage to jump in between those two who, I realized much later, had been trying to kill each other long before I was ever born.

In the course of writing my first book, *From Foster Care to Millionaire,*

I thought about these incidents for the first time in years. I had never seen a reason to dredge up the past, but there I was, writing a book over a period of about three years, thinking of these long forgotten experiences of my past. But this time, there was no emotion attached. It was as though I was thinking of someone I used to know; I was able to look at the situation from a more objective point of view. I asked myself, "If this story was about some other little girl, what would I think of her?" My immediate observation was that it took enormous courage for that little girl to stand between the abused and the abuser, diverting the attention onto herself. From that point on, I was able to see myself in a different light—as the strong, courageous person I am.

As I reflect on the various events in my life, I can see how the courage that developed in the little girl I used to be has served me well in my adult life. When I left my perfectly good job of nearly seven years to start my own company, with no guarantee of survival or success, an outside observer would have thought me crazy. Here I was, leaving a good job with a steady paycheck to start my own insurance agency—it made no sense at all. I had no training in running a business. I didn't know how to keep books, get insurance company appointments, set up an office, or do any of the other things necessary for the successful establishment and growth of a business. But for me and the others like me, who have been through so much, I knew that nothing could happen to me in my own business that would come close to the pain I'd experienced in childhood. If a prospect didn't want to buy his or her insurance from me, that rejection wouldn't leave a scar or a bruise; it wouldn't make me bleed. Rejection is part of business, and for those of us who've experienced what may be the ultimate rejection—rejection by the people responsible for bringing us into the world—all other rejections may hurt, but they are insignificant compared to the hurt we experienced when we were tender and truly vulnerable.

I realize now that I used the courage I learned as a child to leave my job, in the hopes of finding something more fulfilling. It took courage to sit politely and listen to my boss list all the things I didn't know how to do when I gave him notice that I planned to leave his company to start my own business. It took courage to listen to him laugh as he told me that he might consider giving me my job back after my company failed and I was left flat on my face. As he tried to discourage me from doing what he thought was certain failure, I thought: *You don't even know me. You have no idea what I've been through in my life. You can't hurt me. You have no idea how strong I am, how resourceful I am, and how persistent I can be when I set my mind to do something.* After I thanked him for the opportunities he'd given me and for all I'd learned there, I left that meeting determined to dig ditches in the hot sun during the day and wash dishes at night before I would ever go crawling back to work for that company.

That was in 1989. Since then, I have built and sold two successful companies, both of which have helped to protect and defend the good people and organizations that care for children who have been abused. I have endured some significant setbacks, but I'm confident that the courage and other characteristics I learned as a little girl were exactly what I needed to be successful in business.

Successful survivors find meaning in their lives. They are not superficial or shallow. Their thinking tends to run deeper than most people's; having experienced trauma, they are not people who go about living happy-go-lucky lives. Successful survivors need to find purpose and significance to their lives in order to make sense of what they've been through; and once they've found it, they *know* that they do have intrinsic value, and that nothing and no one can ever take that away from them.

Successful survivors refuse to give anyone the power to ruin their lives. They may have been victims in the past, but they have made the shift to seeing themselves as courageous, victorious people, and they are determined never to go back.

When people, activities, or bad habits are holding successful survivors back from reaching their goals, they eliminate the detrimental or toxic elements from their lives. Like pruning branches off a tree so that the remaining branches can thicken and grow full, they limit or entirely cut off the time spent with people and activities that aren't good for them. They know that even if they have to spend time alone for a while, their lives will be fuller in the long run—more rewarding and worth whatever sacrifice they have made. The willingness to assess objectively the people and activities in their lives *and* to take actions that cause them short-term pain will pay off for them in the long run—but it *does* require a tremendous amount of courage.

The quintessential example of acting courageously and finding meaning in life is seen in the life of Tom Monaghan, billionaire and founder of Domino's Pizza—and former foster child. After his father died when he was 4 years old, little Tommy Monaghan was left in an orphanage by his mother. Rather than being bitter and resentful, he credits the nuns in the orphanage for implanting in him a strong sense of integrity, as well as a deep faith in God.

Tom later lived and worked on "the foster farms," as he calls them. He speaks fondly of his time of working on the farm, where he developed a love of agriculture and an understanding of the value of hard work. There were lots of life lessons on the farm, starting with the knowledge that we reap what we sow. Tom Monaghan learned that if you plant corn, and water and fertilize the soil, you'll get a harvest of corn. In other words, you'll never get beans by planting corn. He also learned that, when you fail to do the work and plant nothing, nothing is all you'll get. These basic lessons can be applied for the "harvests" of good things we hope to have throughout our lives.

After aging out of the foster care system, Tom spent three years in the Marines, an experience he still recommends to young men today. As of this writing, Tom is in his 70s, yet still does 150 pushups and 250 sit-ups every other day. The discipline he learned in the orphanage, reinforced on the farm and perfected in the Marines, has stayed with him all of his life. That discipline served him well when he bought his first little pizzeria, sleeping on the floor under the pizza table when he couldn't afford to rent a room. It took courage to scrape up the $500 he needed to buy the business (after a con man had scammed him out of the money he'd saved while in the Marines). It took both courage and tenacity to stay with the pizzeria when it didn't produce enough income to rent a room. And it took courage, along with all the other characteristics of successful survivors that he had acquired through adversity, to build that little pizza place into a billion-dollar, worldwide empire.

And once Tom Monaghan had achieved extraordinary success, he began shifting from success to significance. After deciding on a course for the second half of his life, he acted on his conviction by selling his jets, his collection of 24 Frank Lloyd Wright homes, and other luxuries that he considered superfluous, all to build Ave Maria University and the town surrounding it, Ave Maria, Florida. He founded Legatus (a Latin word meaning *ambassador*), an organization made up of Catholic business leaders, intended to help support and encourage business people to lead with integrity. He also founded the Thomas More Law Center, a nonprofit public interest law center that provides pro bono legal help to people fighting issues that threaten Christian beliefs and values.

By the time I interviewed Mr. Monaghan, he had already given away more than 95 percent of his wealth, all for the purpose of helping others to find God and to gain the education necessary to fulfill their life's purpose. I didn't ask him this question, but I wondered after the interview if it had taken courage to give so much wealth away. People who have grown up lacking the bare necessities tend to want to hang onto what they've accumulated. But Mr. Monaghan gave his money away happily, considering it not a donation, but rather an investment in the only thing that he believes will go on after this life—people.

Other billionaires have told Mr. Monaghan about their plans to use their accumulated wealth to end various diseases, to which he replies, "But the people who don't die of that disease will eventually die of something else, and they will be faced with either heaven or hell. I want to help them get to heaven." Like so many other successful survivors of neglect, abandonment, and abuse, Tom Monaghan has been driven by strong faith, demonstrated in measurable actions. Like many other survivors who have gone on to have careers in serving others, Mr. Monaghan has found meaning in helping others.

There isn't a hint of self-pity in any of Mr. Monaghan's recollections of his time in foster care or the events that led to him being there. It must have taken courage to face the fears brought on by uncertainty, after experiencing the pain of losing his father and being abandoned by his mother. It surely took courage to dismiss any ugly memories and feelings in order to press through to success, and it must have taken courage to give away his wealth for the greater good, but he developed the courage to fulfill the good plan for his life—and the rest of us can too!

FIVE SUCCESSFUL SURVIVAL STRATEGIES:
Courage

What is holding you back? What are you afraid of? Ask yourself, "*If I try this, what's the worst thing that can happen?*" Chances are, the consequences of a failed attempt are insignificant compared to what you've already experienced in your life. Ask yourself, "*How can I maximize my chances of success?*" And then...*take action*. If you are unsuccessful, analyze your results; ask yourself how you can do this differently, and then *try again*. Refuse to let fear hold you back, by doing what you need to do even while you're afraid.

Write a letter to the individuals who have harmed you. Tell them how you feel about what they did. You can destroy it when you're done; you don't have to send it, or allow anyone else to read it. But it's important to get this out of you. Until you say what you want to say, those words will be stored up in you like a poison, one that will eat away at you, eventually stealing your health and your happiness. Once you've gotten all of that stuff out of you, let the anger, bitterness, and resentment go with it. Forgive the harm done; determine right now not to give one more moment of your life over to the negative events of the past. You may eventually get to a place where you can be grateful for those past ugly situations, when you can recognize them as having been catalysts, affording you a deeper level of maturity and a greater level of significance.

Make a list of the toxic people and situations in your life. Next to each item on the list, answer the question, "*How can I eliminate or minimize my exposure to toxicity here?*" For example, if someone is mistreating you, consider giving that person an ultimatum like, "*I care for you, but if you continue to criticize me, I'll have no choice but to distance myself from you.*" If the offending person is a boss, or a relative for whom you are responsible, and you can't limit your exposure to the person, consider all your alternatives. For example, search for a new job or seek an alternative caregiver for the relative. Or you can do what Supreme Court Justice Ruth Bader Ginsburg advised me to do, "*Develop selective deafness. Pretend you didn't hear the offensive remark.*"

What are you really passionate about? If you're not sure, think of any activities that so engross you that you lose track of time. Or, is there something that you've always *wanted* to do? Perhaps your passion lies in those causes that are a reflection of some part of your life story, like child abuse, animal cruelty, or the plight of the homeless. Consider what you know how to do. Ask yourself how you could make time to do the things you love doing, or else ask yourself which of your skills, talents, or abilities you could use to help relieve the suffering you see around you. Determine to make time to apply yourself to your passion. The return on your investment of time will be the firing up of your passion, which can lead to a turning point in your life. Dr. Lawrence LeShan has asserted in his book, *Cancer As a Turning Point*, that when we engage our passion, we give our immune system a reason to do its job to heal and strengthen our bodies.

Before you can nurture hope, you have to be clear on what it is. Hope is very different from a wish. Wishful thinking is just that— thinking, without the energy and action to make it reality. Hope, on the other hand, carries an expectancy. Nurturing hope involves daring to expect that things will get better. The best way to nurture hope is to envision the outcome you would like to see. For example, if a loved one is on drugs, envision him or her healthy, happy, and delivered completely from addiction. If you are suffering with an illness, visualize yourself healed, whole, and energetically pursuing your aspirations. Until you have a clear vision for your good future, you'll have a difficult time engendering hope. Give yourself permission to daydream clearly about the life you want to live. Ask yourself how you can make it a reality in your life. Take action on the leadings you perceive, and then *expect* good things to happen.

SUMMARY

Instead of focusing of what others have done to you or failed to do for you, on what you *could* have done or *should* have done, or on how you may have failed to meet the challenges in your life, let go of all that and choose to give yourself credit for the courage you have exhibited in the difficult situations you've lived through.

Courage helps successful survivors learn to trust others, even when all their instincts tell them never to trust anyone again. Courage enables us to take the risks involved in going where we've never been, and doing things we've never tried. In the face of the risk of rejection, failure, or humiliation, successful survivors summon the courage to try anyway. It's this courage that empowers our persistence, our resilience, and all the other characteristics of successful survivors.

Regardless of whether you *feel* especially courageous or not, know that courage is the undercurrent of the other characteristics of successful survivors which, woven together, have made you who you are.

KEY POINTS FOR DEVELOPING COURAGE

- Don't wait until you "don't feel fear" before you do something to move you forward. Go ahead and do it, even while feeling afraid. Act courageously whether you feel like it or not.
- Forgive those who've hurt you. By refusing to forgive, you continue to give the person who hurt you power over your present and future. Quit looking in the rear-view mirror; turn around and look out the windshield toward your future.
- Eliminate (or severely limit) the time you spend with toxic people or in toxic situations.
- Find meaning in your life and in your future. Your meaning and passion can be found at the intersection of what you care about and what you know how to do.
- Refuse to give up on the good life that awaits you. Nurture hope.

CHAPTER 7

Conscientiousness

CONSCIENTIOUS: desiring to please, self-directed, goal-driven, scrupulous, purposeful, dependable, and dutiful

---

DARREN HARDY, PUBLISHER of *SUCCESS* magazine, spoke in an interview of how his mother had given him away to his father at a very young age. She never returned. His father was a former university football coach who was something of a task master, giving out only hard-earned approval. Darren worked hard to please his dad all through his childhood, and he's been working hard ever since.

Darren doesn't elaborate on the abandonment by his mother, but having been abandoned by my own mother, I can speak to the "primal wound" left in the soul by being unwanted by the woman who gave birth to you. Despite the fact that some people who experienced abandonment know—intellectually, at least—that their biological mothers gave them up specifically because they loved their children, and believed that someone else would be better able to give them what they need, there is still always a wound. Even with loving, adoptive parents, there may always remain something missing, something that is so primal as to be indefinable.

People like myself, Darren Hardy, and countless others often go through life trying to fill that indefinable hole in our hearts, left by the mother whom we perceive as not wanting us. Some of us try to fill the hole with constant activity or with the unending noise of the people we surround ourselves with. Some of us self-medicate; some of us strive to earn the approval of those who *are* around us. I suspect that, like me and countless others, Darren Hardy has tried to fill the hole in his life with the approval of his father, a man who didn't easily dole out approval.

When Darren was only 20 years old, he got into residential real estate sales. It was the early '90s, and the real estate market was tough even for people who had years of experience and built-in clientele. Darren knew nothing about the real estate business: He had no prior experience, clientele, or even credibility. Yet in just 90 days, he was outselling an entire office of 44 veteran agents—combined! *How?* Simple: Darren would park his car, mentally prepare himself for rejection, and start knocking on doors. Regardless of how many doors were slammed in his face, how many angry jeers and barking, biting dogs he faced, he refused to give himself to permission to stop until he had knocked on at least 50 doors.

His deep need to be wanted and approved of drove Darren to become a hard worker, determined to succeed. And succeed he has! Author of the New York Times best-seller *The Compound Effect* and *Living Your Best Year Ever*, Darren has produced more than 1,000 television shows and events, is a motivational speaker, mentors CEOs, advises many large corporations, serves on the board of several companies and nonprofit organizations, encourages people to launch their own businesses, and publishes *SUCCESS* magazine every month, filled with interviews with people like Richard Branson, Warren Buffett, Donald Trump, Howard Schultz (Starbucks), Charles Schwab, Jeff Bezos (Amazon), and many more.

Darren is the quintessential self-motivated hard worker, someone who is determined to prove their worth. Like many conscientious successful survivors of abandonment and other trauma, Darren exhibits the qualities of being ultra-responsible, dependable, accountable, competent, trustworthy, and loyal. The value of good work ethic is indisputable. The term *survivor work ethic* was coined to describe the underlying drive, desire, and actions to prove one's worth and value on the job. **People with a good work ethic are far less likely to be out of work, regardless of what is going on in the economy. They are typically the first ones promoted and the last ones laid off.**

Similar to survivor work ethic is *immigrant work ethic*. Around the turn of the last century, immigrants to this country quickly gained a reputation for their strong work ethic. Grateful even for the opportunity to earn a fair wage by doing honest work, they typically worked longer hours with greater effort and fewer complaints than did people born in the United States. Today, many immigrants value the opportunities available in the United States, much more so than people who were born and raised here. These newcomers are still often found working long hours, trying to earn their piece of the American dream for themselves and their families.

One truly amazing example of a successful survivor immigrant who has worked hard to earn the American dream is in the life of one of the most successful realtors in the United States, Jacqueline Thompson. When Jacqueline was just a little girl, her mother desperately wanted to get her family out of Vietnam. The family's property and savings had all been seized by the Communist government and Jacqueline's mother felt there was no hope for her children to have a good life there. For years, Jacqueline's mother lived very frugally, taking only very small amounts of money out of the bank so as not to arouse the attention of the government officials, who monitored all withdrawals. Eventually she was able to save enough money to pay the way for black market operatives to sneak her family out of the country. She wanted to go to America, but what she had saved wasn't enough to get them all the way. With only the clothes on their back the day they left, they went as far as the little bit of money would take them, and found themselves in a refugee camp in Indonesia.

As a very young girl, Jacqueline remembers rising very early in the morning to go with her mother to try to sell sweet rice cakes to the locals. Because they couldn't speak the language, Jacqueline's mother would sit on the side of the road with her head down and arms lifted high holding the rice cakes up to passersby. When someone would take a rice cake from her hands, they would drop some coins. Jacqueline's mother would use the few coins they earned to meet her family's basic needs, and somehow she also managed to set a little aside to get her family to the United States. This difficult life went on day after day for months, until finally a professor at Cal Poly Pomona sponsored them into the United States, and a Catholic Church in Chino, California, provided the family a small house to stay in until they were able to get on their feet.

Jacqueline's mother's dream of getting her children into the United States of America had finally come true.

Jacqueline and her 11 brothers and sisters were enrolled in school without knowing a single word of English. They worked doubly hard to learn English in addition to the material being taught. They walked or took the bus everywhere they went. The kids applied themselves to their school work, as everyone worked at whatever work they were able to find. It wasn't long before all 19 residents of that little house behind the church (Jacqueline, her siblings, parents, four cousins, and her uncle and aunt) were able to move out into two larger houses.

At 13 years old, Jacqueline got a part-time job after school. At 16, she left her family and moved to Los Angeles, where she enrolled in classes at Santa Monica City College. She worked two, sometimes three jobs to put herself through school and to pay all her own expenses. She consistently outpaced all the other sales people in every job she held—always through doing everything she could to meet the needs of customers.

Eventually, Jacqueline was accepted into the University of Southern California Business School. The only condition was that she provide a copy of her high school diploma. But she didn't have a diploma, as she had left high school before graduating. Being the resourceful, hard-working person she is, Jacqueline went back to the school district to take the test to earn her GED. She was told that she'd have to go to classes for months before taking the test. She didn't have months, and asked for an exception to be made, allowing her to take the test without the classes. It was a unique request and, given the circumstances, they agreed to let her take her GED exam so that she could officially be accepted to USC.

Needless to say, she passed the test and went on to do well in all her studies at USC, all while working full time. Immediately after graduation from the University of Southern California, Jacqueline was hired by Arthur Andersen in their Business Consulting division, as a consultant to Fortune 500 companies. She enjoyed the work, but it wasn't long before Jacqueline wanted more. By this time, Jacqueline had gotten married, and she and her husband decided to open a beauty supply business. With her commitment to finding and fulfilling the needs of her customers, their beauty supply and skin care business thrived. But it wasn't long before Jacqueline was enticed into yet another new business, that of luxury real estate. She did her research and found the most successful realtor in south Orange County. She emailed him—as reserved and graceful as Jacqueline is, she can be very bold—and told the well-known realtor her qualifications, what she thought she could do for his business, and that if he didn't hire her, he'd be making a mistake! He hired her within days of her bold, unsolicited approach to him.

Jacqueline started selling real estate in the highly competitive coastal Orange County area of Southern California. Before long, Jacqueline's work ethic and conscientious approach to maintaining the highest standard of service had earned her the distinction of being one of the most successful, trusted and sought-after realtors in what is often referred to as the California Riviera.

Because of her work ethic, her gratitude for the opportunities present in the United States, and her determination to succeed by meeting the needs of her customers, Jacqueline went from living in a refugee camp and selling rice cakes at the side of the road to being a multimillionaire at the top of her field.

When asked if she had any advice for people who want to succeed, Jacqueline Thompson said, "Be driven, dedicated, and focused. Do the work necessary to become an expert in your area. Stick with it even when you don't seem to be getting results, and eventually, if you don't give up, your hard work will pay off."

Successful survivors have an indefatigable drive to work hard, achieve and succeed, because the positive feelings that result from accomplishment of a task help to build self-esteem and fill the feeling of emptiness that can often follow trauma. There are myriad reasons why children who have experienced hardship are driven to succeed as adults, ranging from a desire for revenge (hence the old saying, "The best revenge is the life well lived.") to a desire to provide one's loved ones with all the things they didn't have when they were children. The underlying nature of their motivation, however, is unquestionably to prove their worth—to themselves, to the ones they love, and to the people or circumstances that let them down or hurt them. Because many successful survivors tend to think they're not good enough, regardless of how amazing they may be, they work hard to prove that they are worthy and to earn the acceptance and approval of others. Consequently, they make excellent employees—sometimes with great personal sacrifice.

Successful survivors want (and often need) love, acceptance, and approval so desperately that they will nearly work themselves to death in an effort to get it. Because of their need for acceptance and approval, they will often be the first ones on the job and the last ones to leave. They will sacrifice their personal relationships and even their health working long hours, striving for acknowledgement, acceptance, and appreciation.

For some, the decision to work long hours is an attempt to maintain a distance from those in their personal lives. This was the case with me. For many years, I worked 80–100 hours a week because I had a deep desire to prove that I was good for something. I grew up hearing, time and again, that I was "good for nothing." I had no idea how to be in a healthy relationship. Where personal relationships were concerned, it was far easier for me to work than to spend time with people in the context of personal relationship. When I *did* spend time with others, it was only a matter of time before I'd say the wrong thing, hurt someone's feelings, or get hurt myself. It was just easier to use my work to maintain distance from friends and family.

Knowing I was doing a good job for a worthy cause made me feel better about myself. My self-esteem rose with every paycheck I earned. Plus, I got to enjoy the reputation I had earned as a hard worker. That label helped to replace some of the ugly labels that had been put on me as a child. The more my clients, co-workers, and associates referred to me as "a hard worker" and "someone who gets the job done," the harder I worked to reinforce and build that reputation.

In our culture, being a workaholic is one of the last socially acceptable ways in which a person's life can be totally out of balance while still being respected. In other words, our society frowns on drug addicts, alcoholics, and people who are addicted to porn, food, hoarding, or any other kind of addiction. However, when people's lives are thrown totally out of balance through an addiction to their work, our culture generally finds it admirable. People compliment workaholics on their exemplary work ethic. I am a great example of this: When I was a young mom, I was respected by others for working hard to provide my child with all the things I didn't have. We lived in a nice home in a safe community. My daughter had all the right clothes and shoes, she went to a private school, and she was able to participate in activities that had been entirely out of the question for me when I was her age.

What I didn't understand clearly back then was that I had arranged my life in a way that allowed me to do what I did well—work, while minimizing the time spent in what I didn't do well—relationships. I had been abandoned and abused in my childhood, so I didn't know how to have healthy relationships with good people. And unfortunately, never having seen good parenting, I didn't know how to be a good mother. I knew I didn't want to harm my child, so I threw myself into my work— not only to gain the acceptance I craved, but to avoid the relationships I felt incapable of nurturing. I wasn't physically abusive to my daughter, but because I seemed to see her as an extension of myself, I was critical of her, constantly prodding her to do better. I never celebrated what she did well; I only pushed her to improve and to strive. That's what I did to myself, and I was unwittingly doing that to her. It wasn't until much later that I learned just how much pressure I had put on her.

Consequently, although my daughter knew I loved her, she didn't feel emotionally safe with me. She didn't confide in me and wasn't entirely comfortable around me. She knew she had to be on guard around me, because sharing anything was opening the door to a lecture (at best) and criticism and discipline (at worst). I never intended to make her feel bad; my intention was to get her to *want* to do better. I had not yet untangled the wiring in my brain that was leading me to believe I was somehow doing her a disservice if I failed to point out every area for possible improvement. I didn't know then the value of identifying her strengths and pointing them out to her to help her build confidence and to feel good about herself.

Those who have had negative labels affixed as children—*orphan, foster kid, disabled, retarded, fat, ugly, unwanted, unloved, sick, burdensome, different,* etc., tend to strive for the good feeling that comes of replacing those labels with the new ones they create for themselves. Being known as "the honest, capable, hard-working, employee" or "the one who's always on time" or "the best bookkeeper" or "the top sales person" or "the best customer service representative in the company" means so much more to successful survivors than it does to those who have a healthy self-image. Therefore, they are often reluctant to draw boundaries at work or to do anything that could jeopardize the positive reputation they have developed as adults. Unless they are replacing their label with another positive label, there is a vague, underlying fear that the loss of the good characteristics they have become known for would leave them with no identity at all.

For many, the overworked, out-of-balance life becomes a lifestyle unto itself. Some employers, who at first appreciated the extra effort from successful survivors, become accustomed to it. They expect these workaholics to continue to reach higher goals, to accomplish more. Those who fail to build themselves up from the inside and who continue to rely on the external approval of others will often exhaust their bodies, driving themselves into an early grave.

Many of us have known people who are highly successful in their chosen field but whose personal lives are in shambles. Sadly, many survivors of trauma never find the balance of good relationships, health, peace, joy, and financial stability that make up real success. They build emotional walls, keeping themselves at a safe distance from others— thereby keeping themselves at a distance from a fuller measure of success. Having all five points of genuine success involves knowing that you are valuable, lovable, and acceptable. When we truly feel worthwhile, when we realize that we *deserve* a good life, we no longer feel the sort of emptiness and pain that is too often filled with the things people frequently use to self-medicate: food, drugs, shopping, one wrong relationship after another.

Successful survivors work hard to earn what others feel entitled to. For example, when I was a little girl, my grandparents and I often didn't have enough to eat. To compound that challenge, food was often used as a reward or punishment. Consequently, I spent many years feeling that I had to somehow earn the right to eat. I have known other adult survivors of trauma who experienced similar feelings about having their own bed to sleep in, a pillow that wasn't stained with the tears and sweat of others, or their own special blanket. Because of this feeling of having to earn what most people take for granted, successful survivors tend to work harder, accomplish more, care more about the quality of their work, and hope for recognition from the people in their lives.

In an effort to seek recognition and to prove that they deserve to be here, to be alive, that they deserve the food they eat and the air they breathe, successful survivors will pick up additional shifts or do work others won't, while looking for ways to compete for the favorable attention of the boss. Conscientious successful survivors are eager to please; they tend to be courteous, helpful, cheerful, humorous, and optimistic. Successful survivors stay above the gossip and politics that often define workplace conversations. They deeply desire someone to be proud of them; they desperately want to hear, "Well done!" Conversely, they can be very difficult bosses (and parents) because they expect others to step it up and perform the way they do—faster, more efficiently, to perfection. Successful survivors tend to have a reputation for being intolerant of anything that (to them) even resembles "slacking off."

Those who were burdened as children with the very adult responsibilities of taking care of their younger siblings or incapacitated parents, of keeping the secrets of abuse or of trying to keep dysfunctional people happy, often become ultra-responsible adults. This can be a good thing, as in the case of the workplace. Successful survivors typically take care of what they see needs to be done without being told to do so. Because they dealt with adult issues and handled adult responsibilities at early ages, many successful survivors are exceptionally good at prioritizing and organizing their thoughts, their personal lives, and their work. Also, because resourcefulness frequently accompanies responsibility, they often don't need a great deal of instruction or supervision in the workplace. This doesn't guarantee that they will always do things in the most efficient manner, but they can usually be counted on to take action and figure out some way to get the job done. As a result, many of them rise to supervisory or leadership roles.

The sense of responsibility found in successful survivors often extends beyond what they are individually responsible for on the job. In a positive light, it can extend to a desire for the company they work for to be profitable. Because of the trauma they've experienced, they often have the perspective that if circumstances are good for the whole, they will be good for the individuals involved. Successful survivors therefore tend to do their part to contribute to the bottom line, for the good of all. In a negative light, this sense of responsibility can result in successful survivors bearing burdens that aren't theirs to bear. If they don't keep a proper perspective, they will worry about things that aren't within their purview, things they can do nothing about.

Closely related to the characteristic of being responsible and conscientious are the characteristics of being loyal and dependable. These qualities seem to go hand-in-hand when successful survivors feel like a valued member of a team. Although this is an extreme example, a young woman who has been taken in by a trafficker after being homeless, given food, clothing, and a place to stay, will often feel a sense of loyalty to the trafficker for having "rescued her" from homelessness. Imagine the sense of loyalty given to a business owner who offers a trauma survivor their first chance to prove themselves on the job.

Because of their strong sense of loyalty, successful survivors can usually be depended upon and trusted. Most of them wouldn't even consider doing anything to harm an employer, especially one who has given them the dignity afforded by a fair wage for honest, honorable work. In fact, they're typically the first ones to defend the actions of an employer; or, at the very least, to give the employer the benefit of the doubt, and encourage others to do the same.

Another aspect of the successful survivors' conscientiousness is self-control. They have learned to make use of a "filter" to keep their thoughts from falling straight out of their mouths. They have the ability to hold back in saying what they would really like to say, like telling off an insulting boss, or to keep from doing what they might imagine doing, like slapping an irritating client. Learning how to survive trauma teaches successful survivors how to smile when they felt like screaming, and how to keep focused on the work at hand while circumstances around them seem out of control.

Healthy people gravitate toward people they like. Those who were traumatized by abuse or rejection tend to gravitate toward people who they *think* like them. Note the difference: Traumatized people need affirmation, love, and a sense of belonging, but unfortunately many of the people whom survivors of trauma gravitate toward don't like them in a healthy way. These people *act* as though they like the conscientious survivor so that they can use them for what the survivor can do for them. It's not difficult to see why so many young girls wind up in the arms of men who mistreat them, or with traffickers who have persuaded them that they are part of "the family." It's also why so many young boys join gangs—it gives them a sense of belonging, albeit distorted.

Not every example is so obvious. Some people try to "earn their belonging" by being the person in a group of friends who is always there for everyone else, which often results in their being taken advantage of. In some cases, the conscientious employee redoubles their efforts to go above and beyond the boss's expectations time and again. Of course, there is nothing wrong with being a good friend or an employee with a good work ethic. But when you are consistently stretching the definition of good friendship, or your strong work ethic goes unrecognized and uncompensated for years (and your health suffers because of it), it's time to re-evaluate the situation.

Conscientious people know that something can be learned from everyone, even if it is how *not* to act and what *not* to do. They know to make the deliberate decision to learn something from every person with whom they interact, so they're always observing others. Successful survivors should not become subservient, but should look for opportunities to be a student to those who can be teachers in their lives. This willingness to learn from others helps successful survivors maintain a sense of humility, a common trait of truly successful people.

Humility, as well as the ability to take correction and receive instruction, are integral to conscientiousness, and can benefit successful survivors in a number of ways. First, the ability to receive correction and instruction with a good attitude allows them to remain more objective in situations that get heated or contentious. Second, it provides an opportunity for them to find the good in other people. They may have to dig a little deeper with some people than with others, but there is good in almost everyone. When successful survivors find the good in a person, they are typically able to have more patience with that person, to articulate the good they've found and thereby build up the person and strengthen the relationship—and perhaps even defuse conflict.

Third, seeing everyone around them as a potential teacher helps successful survivors to continually improve. When they notice something good about someone else, they can work to incorporate those good qualities or behaviors into their lives. Regardless of their age or accomplishments, conscientious people want to continually improve. And finally, when successful survivors view every situation as an opportunity to learn, they are less likely to allow people to ignite the frustration or anger in themselves. Keeping their cool and remaining objective in the midst of a potentially volatile situation helps successful survivors build and maintain good relationships, which makes them extremely valuable in the workplace.

It never feels good to take correction, but successful survivors respect those who have the courage to correct others and who care enough to invest the time in sharing their wisdom and advice. A real friend tells you when you have lettuce in your teeth, when your zipper is down, or when you are wearing something that detracts from your appearance. Only fools resist correction. A wise person receives advice, weighs it based on the character and expertise of the person giving it, dismisses the bad, and incorporates the good into his or her life, becoming a better person as a result. Even in situations where the correction comes from someone you don't respect, and even if you decide not to implement the advice, you can still receive the correction gracefully. It's all right to smile and thank the person for caring enough to take the time to share his or her thoughts, knowing full well that the advice given doesn't apply to your present circumstances.

Successful survivors invest their own time in learning about the company they work for (or the company they wish to work for)—its products or services, the industry, the competition, and other issues that could affect their employment. They know that to be "in the know" is to be a valuable employee. The more value a person brings to their employer, the less likely they are to experience the loss of a job. To the contrary, the more knowledgeable, helpful, cheerful, willing, teachable person may even be promoted over more qualified people who have poor attitudes. Good employers know that they can teach skill sets to employees who have a good attitude, and that it is far more difficult to teach good attitude to a person with a bad attitude who is otherwise highly skilled.

A skill common to conscientious successful survivors of chaos and dysfunction is the ability to "read" the body language of others, detecting the slightest change in voice inflection or facial expression. They sense when people are agreeing with them or pulling away. They are sensitive to the pain of others and to injustice against others. Successful survivors also have what I call an acute "weasel meter," which sounds an alarm in their heads when they perceive that someone is insincere, disingenuous or deceptive in any way. It's not difficult to imagine how valuable this ability is in dealing with customers, vendors and co-workers. Irate customers can be assuaged by an employee who can discern the true source of their irritation. Reluctant buyers can be won over by the employee who can pick up on what specific areas of a product may appeal to the buyer, or else zero in on the buyer's true objections to the sale. And co-workers are more efficient and effective in their work when they feel valued by someone who truly understands their issues. Having learned how to survive the challenges of their lives, successful survivors can use those abilities to handle objections, address concerns, make the sale, resolve conflicts, and ultimately to make friends out of previously skeptical or disgruntled coworkers and customers.

The ability to read people and situations helps successful survivors discern who is with them, who is against them, who can be trusted, and who must be avoided. Many use these skills without even realizing it, but one successful survivor, who prefers to remain anonymous, has capitalized on it as a professional jury advisor to legal teams. She sits in as an observer and watches potential jurors, noting microexpressions and body language that most people miss. She's had no formal training in body language or in law, but her expertise in this area is indisputable. She received her "training" in a home where her mother had a revolving door of abusive boyfriends moving in and out throughout her childhood. Her ability to read their faces and body language allowed her to survive, and later to succeed professionally, specifically because of what she'd been through.

Another survivor who has capitalized on his keen ability to read people and situations is Gavin De Becker, author of the national bestseller, *The Gift of Fear*. As a child, Gavin witnessed, and was the subject of, violence in his home. He watched everything and everyone, and he learned to pick up on everything from large movements to the slightest details. Mr. De Becker survived that childhood and gained a practical, working knowledge of the predictors of violence. He has used that valuable knowledge to help protect many people. His firm, Gavin De Becker & Associates, protects people who are at risk, advises clients on the assessment and management of situations that might escalate to violence, and develops strategies for improving safety and privacy. His books and media appearances (including an entire episode of The Oprah Winfrey Show dedicated to teaching people how to use their gift of fear) have helped millions of people to help themselves. Gavin De Becker's work has earned him three Presidential appointments and a position on a congressional committee. He was twice appointed to the President's Advisory Board at the U.S. Department of Justice, and he served two terms on the Governor's Advisory Board at the California Department of Mental Health.

It's simple fact that the desire of successful survivors to be recognized and valued in personal relationships and in the workplace makes them some of the most cooperative, helpful, conscientious people you'll ever know. Conscientious people are willing to share what they have learned through adversity to help others survive and thrive beyond it as they have.

FIVE SUCCESSFUL SURVIVAL STRATEGIES: Conscientiousness

Extraordinary salesman, author, and motivational speaker Zig Ziglar was known for saying, *"You can get everything in life you want, if you'll just help enough other people get what they want."* Find out the goals of your employer. Ask your supervisor, co-workers, and customers what they need. If there is something you can do that will be of service, offer to do it. Putting the needs of others before your own is the first step to developing good work ethic. Try this for 30 days. In a personal journal, note the effort you made, along with the results. Track your progress in this area to figure out what works well, then do more of what you find leads you closer to your goals.

When developing work ethic, and being willing to go above and beyond the limits of your job description by offering to help others, it's easy to go too far and let your life get out of balance. To keep from sacrificing your personal relationships, create healthy boundaries for yourself. For example, if you've offered to help your supervisor with a special project that requires working extra hours, offer to do the extra work at your lunch and break times rather than before or after work, when that additional time away from your family could create a burden at home. Keep your family time as a top priority unless it's a real emergency—and there should be no more than one or two "real emergencies" every year. Keep a journal of the times you've offered to go above or beyond your job duties, the times you've sacrificed time with your loved ones, and what the results were. This will help you find the right balance of personal and professional success.

If you're like me, and you weren't raised in a courteous, polite environment, conscientious behavior may not come naturally to you. If that's the case, seek out someone who does behave that way, and watch how he or she acts. Listen to what he or she says and the way it's said. Listen to tones of voice, watch body language and facial expressions, and do your best to adopt similar behaviors. If you can't find anyone around you who is exceptionally courteous or kind, look for someone on television or in a movie that exhibits these kinds of behaviors. It may feel awkward and uncomfortable when you first begin to adopt these behaviors, but the longer you stick with it, the more natural these actions will become, until one day you will realize that you are genuinely courteous, kind, and polite. To assist yourself in developing these qualities, take a moment before bed each night to review your day, making a note of times when you made an effort to be courteous, polite, or kind. If you make a consistent effort to incorporate this behavior, you will eventually notice subtle (and not so subtle) rewards, both personally and professionally.

Although learning to apply a "filter" to your language can be a very difficult task, it is well worth the effort. Begin to apply a filter by slowing down your conversations. When you feel the urge to respond to something you see or to what someone says, *stop.* Take a breath. That brief action will give your brain time to consider whether or not what you're about to say will make people around you feel good, awkward, sad, angry, etc. As the poet Maya Angelou said, *"People may not remember what you said or what you did, but they will remember the way you made them feel."* You may get a laugh or some other seemingly favorable response to the things you say, but rarely will anyone point out to you the way your words made them really feel. If your comments or jokes make someone feel inferior or inadequate, you lose. At the end of each day, note the times when you said something you wish you hadn't said, and times that you were able to apply your new "filter" and stop yourself from saying something that might make someone feel bad, or that would have revealed too much information about yourself. If you do this daily, you will eventually begin to see an improvement, as your filter becomes a more natural part of your everyday speech. Becoming skilled at using a "communication filter" *will* lead you to personal and professional success.

Become teachable by listening more than you talk. If someone is willing to teach you how to do something, be grateful. Every skill or lesson you learn makes you more valuable in the workforce. If someone is willing to share information with you, listen. You may learn valuable information about an opportunity that you may not hear about from anyone else. If someone is rude or condescending, don't take offense. Rather, ask yourself what could be wrong in his life to make him so irritable. The answer may enable you to disregard inappropriate comments, and possibly even show some mercy. Regardless of what may drive him to the bad behavior in which he engages, ask yourself what you can learn from that person. As is the case with all the other key points and strategies for developing conscientiousness, use your journal to note the times that you learned from someone. List the teacher and the information acquired. Remember: every day that you learn something (even if it is what *not* to do), you become a better person.

SUMMARY

Whether you think of yourself as naturally conscientious or not, you can develop this important characteristic. Begin by striving to be the best you can be. Set goals for yourself. Measure yourself and strive for improvement in everything you do.

Be willing to work hard. Ask questions, read instructions,

and give your best effort at everything you do. Be willing to try new things. If you have an exceptionally difficult task ahead of you, determine to do it first before tackling the other items on your to-do list.

Celebrate your successes. Give yourself credit for failed attempts. Take an honest look at what went wrong; make adjustments, and try again. Draw appropriate boundaries in your personal life and at work. In today's world of declining work ethic and dismal customer service, the successful survivors' conscientiousness—their willingness to do what needs to be done—truly sets them apart.

KEY POINTS FOR DEVELOPING CONSCIENTIOUSNESS

- Develop strong work ethic by finding out what employers and/or customers want. If it's legal and moral and within your ability—DO IT.
- Work hard, but not at the price of sacrificing personal relationships. Schedule time with loved ones if necessary, but don't give everything at work and leave yourself nothing for those you value most.
- Act courteous, polite, helpful, cheerful, and optimistic. If it doesn't come naturally to you, use your words, facial expressions, and body language to act the way a person with those qualities would act.
- Exercise self-control by learning NOT to let every idea that pops into your head fall out of your mouth. Allow only helpful words to leave your mouth; if it isn't helpful to others, don't say it. When you learn to control your words and actions, you'll be well on your way to success.
- See everyone as a teacher, and try to learn something from everyone—even if it means learning how *not* to act! Be willing to take instruction and correction from others. The more you learn, the more valuable you'll be, both to your current and to any future employer.

CHAPTER 8

Resourcefulness

RESOURCEFUL: the ability to improvise to accomplish a goal
or complete a task; figuring out how to make things work
or work things out; exercising one's ingenuity

A S A 15-YEAR-OLD foster kid, Chris Chmielewski was moved
to various foster homes and group homes, where he learned
how to survive the turf wars and bullies all too common to
the foster care system. One evening, Chris smelled smoke. He went out
to investigate and saw that a building was on fire. He could hear the
sirens that indicated that firefighters were on their way and had the fore-
thought to run several blocks to the newspaper office to let them know
about the fire so they could cover the story. He pounded on the door,
but the office was closed. So he ran back to the group home, grabbed
some paper and a pen, ran back to the fire, and wrote the story himself.

Chris did what he thought a "real" reporter would do. He interviewed bystanders and the firefighters who would speak to him. He watched what the first responders did, took note of the time and other specific details, and wrote the story. He printed it out neatly and delivered it to the newspaper editor the following day. No other employee of the newspaper had covered what was a big event in that town, so the editor of the newspaper published Chris' coverage of the event, and a journalist was born.

The fact that the editor of his hometown newspaper valued his work enough to publish it was the encouragement Chris needed to fuel his desire to work his way out of the foster care system, a system that he knew needed to change. Years later, Chris created *Foster Focus* magazine, the only monthly magazine devoted entirely to every aspect of the foster care system. Through his publication, Chris lets the country know what is happening in our nation's foster care system. Foster care leaders provide perspective pieces on the mental, emotional, and physical health challenges kids in the system face. Foster alumni of all ages tell of their experiences without fear of retribution, in the hopes that their transparency and vulnerability will spark needed systemic change. Foster parents voice their frustrations, fears, and triumphs. Perhaps the most rewarding aspect of the work for Chris Chmielewski is when lawmakers take notice and introduce legislation, like the law that made funding available for care and treatment of rescued trafficking victims, many of whom are former foster kids.

Like many entrepreneurs, Chris works long hours. When something breaks, he learns how to fix it. When he wanted to enhance articles with graphics, he taught himself how to add them. When he needed to learn magazine layout, he taught himself how to do that, too. And Chris' resourcefulness doesn't end with his entrepreneurial spirit. He has used his self-taught skills, his colorful personality, and his unflagging commitment to improving the lives of kids everywhere to recruit well respected columnists, to keep the costs of publication affordable for everyone through the sale of advertisements to companies that do business with foster care organizations, and to earn himself a seat at the table of important legislative hearings involving foster care.

Because of his resourcefulness, his ability to communicate and his quick-witted sense of humor, which Chris had used to survive abuse, bullies, and everything else that accompanies being in the foster care system, Chris Chmielewski has earned the support of leaders in foster care throughout the United States. His publication and podcasts are now nationally recognized and seen as valued resources by people in every level of the nation's child welfare system.

Resourceful successful survivors often look at the tough times in their lives as "blessings in disguise," because it is these tough circumstances that force them to figure out how to get through trauma. People who have survived difficult experiences develop coping mechanisms that help them deal with future challenges. Those who haven't been through any serious challenges often don't develop the critical thinking processes necessary to solve problems or create new inventions.

Successful survivors are creative—often out of necessity. For example, a resourceful child left alone at home with nothing more to eat than the remnants of a bag of rice and a dab of ketchup will figure out how to use those two ingredients to ease the pain of hunger. When a resourceful person's car quits running and she doesn't have the money to have her only source of transportation repaired, she is forced into opening the hood, pulling out the manual, and doing her best to figure out how to get the car up and running again.

Much like those who have been deployed into combat zones, those who grow up in abusive environments, where creativity and resourcefulness are necessary to their survival, have received an education that cannot be acquired in a university classroom. With every successfully survived tour of duty, every meal created from next to nothing, every appliance or piece of equipment they somehow manage to repair, and every difficulty they were able to resolve, a successful survivor's confidence in themselves and their ability to survive increases. It's only natural, then, that successful survivors use this resourcefulness, which has been inextricably woven into the fabric of their being, in every situation they face. Because of past successes, resourceful successful survivors are more likely to take things apart to try to figure out what's wrong. They're more likely to break problems down into smaller, more manageable challenges, resolve one challenge at a time, and eventually overcome every adversity. Overall, they are more likely to resourcefully overcome any challenges that come their way.

Resourcefulness is sometimes confused with luck. It is important to distinguish the characteristic of being resourceful from being lucky, because luck, by its definition, is arbitrary. When people fail and chalk it up to bad luck, they are in fact choosing to take no responsibility for their part in the failure. Conversely, when people succeed and chalk it up to good luck, they miss out on the lesson of the factors that worked to yield the good result. Just as we want to learn what *doesn't* work in order to avoid it in the future, it's important to learn what *does* work, so that we can replicate the actions that lead to success.

Dr. Richard Wiseman of the University of Hertfordshire in England teaches that some people who appear quite lucky are *not* "luckier" than others, but rather are more open to random opportunities. This was true in the story above involving 15-year-old Chris Chmielewski, who decided to write the story of the downtown fire "simply" because the local newspaper had no reporter covering the story. Chris hadn't planned to write a story that night; he wasn't a writer. He had never even considered becoming a reporter. He was a kid who had been removed from his family and placed in foster care. He was just trying to live one day at a time, not knowing what was going to happen next. But when Chris smelled smoke and saw that no one was covering the story, he intuitively identified for himself an opportunity to help the newspaper and serve the community. In his openness to this random opportunity, Chris Chmielewski unwittingly launched a career.

Dr. Wiseman states in his book, *The Luck Factor,* that luck is a state of mind, a way of thinking and behaving.[4] He asserts that we have more control over our lives—and our so-called "luck"—than we realize. One study in particular confirmed his assertion: Professor Wiseman handed some study participants a newspaper and asked them to count the number of photographs on its pages. On the second page of the paper, in large, bold font, Professor Wiseman had inserted into the newspaper of every participant a message that read: *Stop counting—there are 43 photographs in this newspaper.* Another message inserted halfway through the paper said: *Stop counting—tell the experimenter you've seen this and win $250.*[4] Now: were the people who noticed this message and collected the $250 lucky? Or were they observant and resourceful?

It's easy to imagine that the college student participants who stopped counting after reading the first message on page two were identified as those most observant and open to opportunities. The ones who saw the second message and collected the $250 were rewarded for their awareness and observation, and the people who took the time to go through the entire paper and count the pictures yet won nothing were understandably disgruntled. After all, they had agreed to participate, had stuck to the original rules, done what was asked, yet suffered the embarrassment of losing to those who appeared to be cleverer than they.

I suspect that the first two groups, those who stopped after reading one of the inserted notes, are most likely to succeed in life. That's not to say that those who strictly follow the rules won't do well. But my assertion comes from my own life experiences, and those of the other successful survivors of trauma I've interviewed. Successful survivors seem to "stumble" into far more of those types of opportunities that seem to randomly present themselves.

For example, when I learned that insurance companies sell the stolen vehicles that are recovered after the vehicle owner has been compensated for his or her loss, I began to buy recovered vehicles, fix them up, and resell them for profit. This was something I did "on the side," after working a full day in the insurance office. Any one of the people I worked with in the insurance agency could have done this, but they didn't. I saw the opportunity and acted on it. Was I "luckier" than my co-workers? No; I was just always looking for opportunities to earn extra money.

When I quit my job and started my first company, some of my well-meaning co-workers expressed their concern for me. What if I failed? Why leave a secure job with salary and benefits? Their comments suggested that the risk I was willing to take was clearly outside of their comfort zone. Having had nothing before that job, I wasn't afraid of the risk. I knew what poverty felt like, and I knew that having worked my way out of poverty before, I could do it again. Later, when it was clear that my business was not only surviving, but thriving, some of these same people expressed their congratulations at my "good luck." While I accepted the well wishes with a polite smile, I was thinking, "Luck? Are you kidding me?! The life I enjoy now is the result of the courage it took to take an enormous, calculated risk, combined with resourcefulness, determination to succeed, tenacity, and 80-plus-hour workweeks!"

Many successful survivors have been labeled by others as "lucky." Dismissing the success of others as mere luck is an effort to lower one's expectations for themselves, thus "letting them" chalk up their own failures to "bad luck." There are lots of old adages that address this issue of luck, such as "We each make our own luck," and, "The harder you work, the luckier you get."

Professor Wiseman says, "Life's best survivors not only cope well, they often turn potential disaster into a lucky development,"[4] which is, perhaps, another way of saying my life's motto, "Succeed because of what you've been through." Professor Wiseman summarized his research by saying, "Luck is a frame of mind, an openness to opportunity."[4]

Being open to opportunity is the first step toward strategic risk-taking—an important aspect of resourcefulness. Successful survivors are willing to take calculated risks. Don't confuse this with gambling. The results of gambling are random and outside of your control. In strategic risk-taking, you control many of the variables. The degree of risk involved in an endeavor is usually a predictor of the possible return on investment. Typically, the higher the risk of loss, the greater the potential return. The converse is also true—the lower the risk, the lower the potential return. Successful survivors are willing to take calculated risks and to use their resourcefulness to make the adjustments necessary to achieve their goals.

Many successful survivors are open to opportunities because they have so little to lose. Sometimes it takes someone with nothing to lose to take the greatest risks. Some of the seemingly goofiest things attempted have become monumental successes, such as Tom Monaghan buying a pizzeria as a young man with no business experience and ultimately expanding his Domino's franchises all over the world; or Harland Sanders driving from restaurant to restaurant trying to sell his fried chicken recipe—the recipe that is now found in tens of thousands of KFC restaurants all over the world.

Resourceful people are compelled to *do something* when they see a problem. While some people turn away and pretend the problem doesn't exist, and others wring their hands and do nothing but complain about it, successful survivors take action. It might not be the *right* action, and it might not resolve the problem entirely, but resourceful people can be counted on to at least try to do something to fix the problem. If there is a leak in the plumbing dripping water under the sink, some people will ignore the problem, hoping it will go away—until the water has caused significant damage and mold has set in. Others will talk about the problem and worry about it, complaining that they don't know what to do about it or that they have no money to get the problem fixed. The resourceful person is the one who clears out the area under the sink, rolls up his or her sleeves, and crawls in there to try to find a solution to the problem.

Smart employers always look for employees who are both resourceful and bold enough to take action when faced with a problem. They respect and reward people who take action to address a problem rather than be paralyzed with indecision or fear. People willing to exercise their ingenuity by trying to deal with the issues of life are far more likely to resolve their challenges successfully than those who won't even try.

Resourceful people don't have all the answers, but they can be counted on to do all they can to find answers to problems. One example of extreme resourcefulness is in the life of an amazing woman who was left homeless after her husband loaded all their things in the family car to move out of state. Before she could get in the car, her husband jumped in and drove away. He literally left his wife and small son on the sidewalk with nothing but the clothes on their backs.

Je'net Kreitner, a talented woman who had enjoyed stage and TV success, was left abandoned and homeless. As a young girl, she had been molested by a babysitter and by her father. But this resourceful, courageous woman didn't give in to self-pity. She did what she had to do to survive and to raise her son. She found a relative who was willing to allow her son to stay during the week so that he'd be able to be in school consistently while Je'net slept in the park or wherever she could find a relatively safe spot—as much as anyone can sleep in a cold, damp, scary place. On the weekends they lived in hotel rooms.

Many people would understandably fall into depression and despair after being left on the street. But Je'net Kreitner didn't give in to sadness, despite all the mistreatment she'd experienced in her life. She continued to look for ways to survive, one day at a time. Ultimately, she worked her way off the streets and started her own nonprofit homeless shelter for women, which she calls Grandma's House of Hope. She helps women whom other shelters have turned down, including women fighting cancer and other life-threatening diseases. Je'net went from barely surviving to thriving, by helping others survive with dignity. Grandma's House of Hope is a testament to her resourcefulness.

Resourcefulness is often accompanied by persuasiveness and leadership. People who roll up their sleeves to attack a problem are sometimes hindered by the people who are invested in ignoring or complaining about the problem. The ability to lead others in collaboration, cooperating to find solutions, is integral to being resourceful—be it persuading a vendor to give you a discount or persuading a loan officer to make an exception. Resourceful people don't always get everything they ask for or achieve everything they attempt, but they know that if they do not ask, they will never receive, and if they do not try, they will never succeed.

FIVE SUCCESSFUL SURVIVAL STRATEGIES: Resourcefulness

Being attentive to one's surroundings doesn't come easily to everyone. The good news is, you can train yourself to look around to see what needs to be done. Make a list now of the things you would like to do, repair, or improve. Keep your eyes open for opportunities, and don't limit yourself to considering only what has been done before. Don't restrict yourself to just what others say you can (or can't) do, or to what others give you permission to do. Just because you've never done something before, doesn't mean you can't do it. Ask yourself, *"How can I improve this situation?"* When you see an opportunity, *act* on it. Don't second guess yourself or try to talk yourself out of it. Muster your courage, and give it your best try.

Review the list of all the things you would like to do, repair, or improve, and add to it any needs of others that you notice aren't being met, or for which there appears to be no ready solution. Next, make a list of all the things *you* could do to address each of these items. Don't judge your ideas; write them all down. Some of your ideas may not make any sense, or they may not be applicable, but do as Walt Disney is known to have done, and consider every possibility, even the seemingly ridiculous ones. Then, after you've exhausted every possible approach, go back through and decide which things to try, and in which order.

Once you have an idea of what to do to help make a difficult situation better or to take advantage of an opportunity, *act*. Don't be like the people who allow fear or failure to keep them from trying. If that's you, ask yourself, "*What's the worst thing that can happen if I fail?*" Chances are that failure won't lead to loss of life! Ask yourself, "*What's the best thing that can happen?*" The answer to this question should overcome any fear. You might realize that you're capable of more than you once thought; you might discover a hidden talent or ability; others may recognize your courage and willingness to tackle a tough problem; there are so many possible positives to the best-case scenario. You never know where your efforts to address unmet needs will lead you—it may even lead right into your real success.

You can increase your chances of "creating your own luck" if you ask yourself every day, "*How can I help someone today? How can I move closer to my goals today? How can I engage my passion today?*" When you start your day by asking these questions, you literally put your brain to work in searching for the answers. As you move through your day, your brain is constantly scanning your surroundings to answer those questions. When you see an opportunity, grab it. Others may chalk your gains up as luck, but you'll know better.

It's a fact that you'll be more willing to try if you learn to accept failure. This may sound counter to the purpose of this book, but the truth is that no one succeeds in every endeavor. But although you may fail at an attempt to do something, in your willingness to try you will develop a reputation as someone who is willing to *do* something, rather than stand around and wait for someone else to tackle problems. This willingness to try can lead to promotions and other opportunities. Trying to help will set you apart from the crowd. And although you may fail from time to time, you will eventually succeed *if* you refuse to give up.

SUMMARY

Being open to opportunity, being willing to take calculated risks, leading others, being persuasive, and being determined to find solutions to problems are all aspects of the attribute called resourcefulness.

Resourcefulness is embodied in the person who, when they see what must be done, rolls up his or her sleeves and begins to take action anyway—despite having no idea how to do it. This is how new inventions come to fruition, new recipes are created, cures are discovered, and new music is composed. Resourceful people may feel fear or anxiety, but they try anyway.

Overcoming the adversities you've experienced likely involved the attribute of resourcefulness. The good news is that resourcefulness is a quality that is developed through trial and error. You can begin right now to develop resourcefulness. Look around for those things in your life that could be improved or that are in need of repair, and consider ways that you might fix or improve them. You may have resourcefulness you haven't yet tapped into. If your efforts don't yield perfect results right away, try again. If you'll approach every problem with an attitude of hopeful resourcefulness, you'll find that you're able to do much more than you thought possible.

Successful survivors understand that the more they try to find solutions to the challenges they face, the more resourceful they become. As you find yourself growing in this area, your resourcefulness and confidence will grow. Starting today, work to see yourself as the resourceful person you are!

KEY POINTS FOR DEVELOPING RESOURCEFULNESS

- Pay attention to your surroundings and circumstances so that you can quickly identify needs and potential challenges. Prompt assessment of the needs of self and others is an identifier of resourceful people.

- As soon as a need or challenge is spotted, develop your critical thinking processes by considering the various ways to address the challenge or solve the problem.
- Be willing to try to take on the challenge of fixing or improving the situation. Resourceful people don't walk away from a problem saying, "That's too bad." Rather, they walk *toward* the problem, willing to try to make the situation better.
- Don't make the mistake of dismissing resourcefulness as luck. Continuously be on the lookout for opportunities to help yourself and others. In so doing, you will be creating your own luck.
- Do *something* to solve problems. Many people back away from problems because they don't know how to fix them. You may not have the answers, and you may not be able to solve the problem right away, but make the decision to be someone who will *try*.

CHAPTER 9

Mine Your Lessons

Mining lessons is the difficult work of digging beneath the surface
of painful events until the nuggets of gold are uncovered.

ALL OF US have experiences in our lives that shape us, for good
or bad. By now, you're hopefully beginning to connect the dots
and see the ways in which your experiences have resulted in
your unique mixture of valuable character traits. The first step toward
really mining the valuable life lessons hidden within the adversities
you've experienced is learning to see your painful experiences in the
light of the mature adult you are now.

One great way to do this is by creating a Lifebook. Your Lifebook is
yours and yours alone; you can choose to share it with others, you can
keep it to yourself, or you can destroy it entirely once you're done with
it. Whatever you ultimately choose to do, don't skip this step—this one
activity can be the turning point that points you toward personal and
professional success.

You can create your own Lifebook using a bound book with blank pages, a scrapbook, lined paper in a binder, anything that you can write on and keep together. You can also create an electronic Lifebook using a word processing or presentation program. Using whichever method you prefer, you'll first separate your Lifebook into three separate sections:

The first section will represent your **past**. This will include those situations you've successfully survived. Recognize that each survived adversity is an accomplishment for which you can give yourself credit. Imagine that every situation you've faced was a test that you successfully passed—because you're still standing!

The second section is your **present**. In this section, you'll focus on what's good about your life now. Don't focus on limitations, what you think you lack, or what others aren't doing for you. Instead, give yourself credit for being in your right mind, being able to think, see, hear, walk, and talk. Imagine a better future; focus on the characteristics of successful survivors that you'll identify within the pages of this book.

The third section will be your **future**. Using this section, give yourself permission to dream about the life you want to live. Consider every facet of your life; create a real vision for what you would like to see as reality in your future, in the areas of personal relationships; health and fitness; peace and joy; and finances. Imagine the home you want to live in, the people you want to spend your life with, the work that makes you feel most alive, and the attitude that makes you feel unstoppable.

In each section, write your own stories or poems; draw pictures, or use works of others; transcribe song lyrics; clip pictures from magazines or postcards that speak to you. The focus of your Lifebook should always be positive—it's *your* story, and you can envision your story the way you choose to. See yourself as a victor instead of a victim—as a conqueror, an overcomer.

The next step toward connecting the dots between the adversity in your life and the valuable characteristics you've developed is in creating an "Adversity/Positive Traits/Advantages" table. On a large sheet of blank paper, create a three-column table. In the far left column, make a chronological list of the major events of your life, from the day of your birth until today. In the middle column, list all of the positive traits you would use to describe yourself. In the third column, use your imagination to consider how your positive traits can help you create personal and professional success. When I do this exercise, my results look like this:

Adversity	Positive Traits	Advantage
Abandoned/alone	independent, self-reliant	equipped me to be an entrepreneur
Physical abuse	empathetic, awareness/ intolerance of injustice	equipped me to be an advocate for kids who have been abused
Homeless resulting from uninsured fire	keen appreciation for insurance and risk management	equipped me to be a proponent for proactive risk management and comprehensive insurance protection
Poverty	resourceful, ability to manage money, desire to help others help themselves rise up out of poverty, gratitude for everything	equipped me to make the temporary sacrifices to start and build businesses, make investments, and to ultimately enjoy long term financial success
Verbal aggression and abuse	courage, resilience, ability to diffuse conflict and hostility	equipped me to deal with difficult people

Now that you've connected your painful experiences to your positive traits and considered the potential advantages, the (very important) next step toward unlocking and unleashing your potential is to learn to love and value yourself as the unique, capable, and powerful person you are. Your exact combination of abilities, talents, skills, and gifts is unique in the entire world. This is not an overstatement; it is scientifically true: your DNA is uniquely different from that of your biological mother, father, siblings, and all other people on earth.

When you value and love yourself, you fill the place in your heart that longs for the love and approval of others. It *is* nice to have the approval and acceptance of others, but you should never depend on it for your personal fulfillment. When you no longer need to find your value in the eyes and words of others, you are truly free—free to make good choices about your life, free to keep and maintain a good, healthy attitude about yourself, and free to live the life you were born to live. In short, when you value yourself, you regain your power; you no longer give control over your power to another person.

You will notice that, when you see yourself in the light of your qualities and potential, others begin to see you differently, too. When that happens, you'll notice that people begin to treat you differently, as you attract good people and new opportunities into your life.

For some people, valuing and loving themselves for who they *are* rather than for what they can *do* is difficult. If that's true for you, begin to value yourself by listing all the personality traits that make you a good person. Consider traits like being a good listener, being honest, loyal, dependable, etc. Consider the ways that you help others (remember that giving someone a genuine smile can be helpful and encouraging!) As you develop characteristics and personality traits, add to your list. Some people benefit from writing positive self-descriptions on photographs of themselves. Photographs, surrounded by descriptive words and printed into posters, can hang in places where they'll be seen daily as a reminder of how valuable you are.

Once you begin to love and value yourself, determine not to give even one more second of your life to painful past experiences. If you focus on past experiences, you allow them to hold you back. If you allow the past to hinder your future, the hurtful people and circumstances have permission to keep on hurting you. In effect, they (along with the awful memories in your mind) "own you." Revoke that permission by putting the trauma where it belongs—in your *past*. Some people find value in writing out the details of their painful experiences and burning them in the fireplace, or tearing up the papers into tiny pieces and flushing them. Some experience release from the control of painful experiences by writing letters to the people who hurt them. Whether or not letters of this nature make it into the hands of the ones responsible for the hurt isn't the point. The point is to get that poison out of the survivor so that the wounds can begin to heal.

The ultimate goal is to get rid of any anger, bitterness, or resentment toward the people who played a role in your painful experiences. The people responsible for your pain may not deserve forgiveness, but forgiveness isn't for them. It's for *you*. Forgiveness doesn't excuse bad behavior or wrong decisions—**by definition, forgiveness is undeserved!**

The truth is that in order to achieve every facet of real success, we must value the lessons we've learned and be grateful for the characteristics developed and honed through those painful experiences.

FIVE SUCCESSFUL SURVIVAL STRATEGIES: Mining Your Lessons

Begin by creating your own personal Lifebook. Write out what has happened to you, as you recall it. As painful as it may be to do this, it's important that you do this step. You can destroy it when you're finished if you choose, but do this for *you*.

Once you've written your story, read through it as though it were the story of a friend telling you what happened to him or her. As objectively as possible, imagine telling your friend that you're sorry about what happened to her. Tell her that you're glad she survived, and then describe to your friend the good characteristics you see in who they are now. This exercise works to change your overall perspective on your past, and can really help to change your outlook for your future. Now, think of three things that you can do to show kindness to yourself every week. This could be getting up an hour early for an hour of quiet time all to yourself, it can be a hot bath, or whatever special treat works for you.

Create your "Adversity/Positive Traits/Advantages" chart by creating a three-column table. At the top of the columns write, "Adversity," "Positive Traits," and "Advantages." In the Adversity column, list the "game-changing" painful events of your life in a few words or even initials that signify the event. In the Positive Traits column, list one of your positive traits or coping mechanisms that may have been acquired or developed through dealing with that adversity. Then in the "Advantages" column, list the possible ways you can use your positive traits. For example, could your positive traits help you in customer service, sales, marketing, caretaking, listening, conflict resolution, etc.?

One way that you can change your paradigm from victim to survivor, or from survivor to successful survivor is to repeat to yourself, *"I'm strong, I'm resilient, I'm resourceful, I'm adaptable, I'm responsive, I'm conscientious,"* **etc.** Refuse to say anything negative about yourself, and refuse to listen to anyone else's negative statements about you. Decide to spend at least five minutes every day telling yourself who you really are. Meditate on these successful survivor characteristics until your way of thinking, and the truth of the successful survivor you are, become inseparable. Some people look at themselves in a mirror as they repeat these statements about themselves. Try it; you cannot do so without smiling. Just this simple act for a few minutes every day can start your day on a positive note.

One way to release negative emotions is to find some time to sit quietly alone, close your eyes, breathe deeply, and visualize each of your negative feelings as chains, literally wrapped around you. For example, anger toward someone who harmed you would be one chain; envy toward someone in your life who was not harmed as you were could be another. You may see one big chain wrapped around you, or you may envision yourself completely bound in chains. Once you've envisioned every negative emotion separately, imagine power bubbling up in you, building to the point that it explodes from you, bursting all those chains so that they disintegrate into dust. The idea here is that you emerge from this exercise a little more aware of your own power to eliminate those negative emotions from your life. You may not think that negative emotions are holding you back, or you may know well that negative emotions have a hold on you, but you feel completely justified in holding on to them. There may even be some comfort in holding onto negative emotions. But if you choose not to do the work necessary to rid yourself of those emotions, you will forever be bound by them, and will not make the shift from survivor to successful survivor. Remember, letting go of negative emotions is about releasing yourself and unleashing your potential. Do this exercise as many times as it takes to break the chains that are holding you back from personal and professional success!

SUMMARY

Do not get this far and put the book down! If you choose not to work through these steps, you cheat yourself, wasting your pain and missing out on the priceless happiness that lies beyond this work. You've already done the hardest part in living through adversity—now it's time to start reaping the benefits.

Following these steps will not lock you into years of therapy or take you back through pain that you cannot bear. Remember that you've already done the work of surviving. Your job now is to take a more objective, even academic, look at your experiences. Just as professional athletes review game tapes to get a different perspective of what happened in a game they've already played and to strategize about what to do differently in the future, successful survivors review their painful experiences, keeping the good and discarding the rest.

KEY POINTS FOR MINING YOUR LESSONS

- *You matter.* Your story matters. Your perspective on the world matters. Do not dismiss the idea of creating your

Lifebook, thinking that you don't want to relive the pain, or that what you have to say is insignificant. What's the point in surviving painful experiences if you fail to mine the lessons out of them? You are better able to put pain behind you for good after you get the story up and out of you.

- Imagine your story as though it were that of a friend, telling you what's happened to him or her. Would you be harsh to a friend who had survived what you've been through? Not likely. We tend to have more compassion toward others than we do for ourselves. Determine to show yourself at least the same amount of compassion and kindness that you would show someone else.

- Considering your painful experiences: What characteristics did you use to survive? How did you cope? Use your characteristics and coping mechanisms to create your own "Adversity/Positive Traits/Advantages" table. Creating this table will help you gain a visual perspective of the connection between the adversities you've experienced and the advantages you have for your successful future. Once you've created your personal table in your Lifebook, look at it often to remind yourself of how far you've come, the characteristics you've developed, and the advantages you've earned. Doing this will spark ideas for putting your advantages to use in creating your good future.

- Give yourself credit for surviving! Value yourself as the strong, capable survivor you are. Love yourself. Be kind to yourself. Take care of yourself.

- Determine to let anger, bitterness, resentment, and every other negative emotion drain out of you. Those negative emotions are chains that lock in your potential. There is no place for those negative chains in your bright future. Give yourself and everyone involved mercy, and in so doing, you will unleash your potential.

CHAPTER 10

The Foundation of Real Success

The foundation of real success is finding and fulfilling the
good plan for which you were perfectly matched,
and enjoying everything that accompanies it

AUTHENTIC SUCCESS ISN'T complete until you engage your passion. Many people live their whole lives with the vague sense that they are not good enough or that authentic success is outside of their reach. Integral to real success are the incomparable feelings found at the intersection of what you love doing and what others need and value. When you are able to support yourself by doing what you love to do, you find yourself in the sweet spot of feeling acceptable and valued for being who you are and for doing what you are uniquely qualified to do. When you find and fulfill the work for which you are perfectly matched, you will feel a sense of satisfaction that you simply cannot attain any other way.

People who have a healthy sense of their worth and value feel good about themselves. They tend to choose better people with whom to develop relationships. They tend to make better life choices, and consequently get better results than those who feel unfulfilled and unvalued. Sadly, those who go through life without that unequaled feeling of being valued and fulfilled, often find themselves in relationships and jobs in which they feel unappreciated or unloved.

Hopefully, this book has helped you to identify the positive qualities about yourself, and helped you to feel more like the awesome person you truly are. **Don't make the mistake of putting this book down without letting these ideas be a turning point in your life. Transformational thinking leads to transformational doing, which results in transformed living.** The concepts, key points, and strategies in this book will change your life. However, in the same way that medication left in the bottle will not treat an illness, work left undone will not change your life. As long as you're breathing, there is still more to learn, there are more lessons to mine, and there is greater depth to your successful survivor characteristics to hone, so keep these ten tips in mind:

10 TIPS FOR DEVELOPING SURVIVAL CHARACTERISTICS

1. Identify your natural survival characteristics and build on them.
2. Cultivate a vivid imagination by taking time to see yourself in the circumstances you desire.
3. Act like the person you want to become.
4. Embrace who you are, and celebrate who you are becoming.
5. Don't make excuses for who you're not.
6. Don't feel sorry for yourself.
7. Avoid substances and behaviors that numb your pain.
8. Prepare for and expect your big break to happen at any time.

9. Choose to have faith in yourself and in something greater than yourself.

10. Mine the lessons out of what you've been through and use them to succeed.

Now that you have identified the characteristics that make you awesome, *engage* those characteristics. Use them in your personal and work life. Talk about your good characteristics, and notice and point them out in others. It's your personality, your strengths, talents, natural abilities, learned skills, and character traits that weave together to form the awesome package that is YOU. That combination is what defines you—not what you own, how much money you earn, or what kind of car you drive. When you begin to truly value and celebrate who you are and what you are capable of, there will be no reason to envy others. You will be able to feel happy for others *without* thinking that they are somehow better or more deserving than you are.

When you are living in that place of "doing what you enjoy while being your authentic self," you will have more of those invaluable things that people seek their whole lives—love, joy, and peace. When you have those things in abundance, those treasures that cannot be diminished by external circumstances, you're better able to show more patience, kindness, gentleness, and forgiveness to others. In other words, you are better positioned to help love others into wholeness.

If you still don't feel awesome, the good news is that you can continue the work of developing these characteristics until you feel a genuine sense of self-worth. You can go back again and again to use the keys and strategies at the end of every chapter to further develop the specific characteristics that will help you survive the challenges that inevitably arise. You can also emulate the characteristics of the people whose stories have been told in this book and those of other successful survivors you may know. Their stories can serve as inspiration for you as you move forward to create an even better you.

You can also create and foster in yourself the feelings of love and acceptance. This is done through establishing healthy relationships with others. Good relationships, on both a personal and professional level, will enrich your life in ways you may not now be able to imagine. What good relationships look like, and how to establish, develop, and maintain them is an enormous subject, but the bottom line for people who have been traumatized is two-fold. First, if you're in relationship now with someone who mistreats you, figure out how to get out of the relationship or how to distance yourself from the toxic person. Making better life choices involves choosing good people to spend time with, ones who will treat you appropriately. Choose the type of person you want in your life, rather than remaining in a bad relationship with someone who you're with by default. You can and *should* do better for yourself. Second, don't expect others to pay for the wrongs done to you by others in the past. Too often, people who have been mistreated destroy good relationships by carrying the attitudes and hurts from the past into the present. Doing this undermines potentially good relationships. The new people in your life are not those people who hurt you; it's unfair to assume that they will mistreat you. Consider how you would feel if everyone you met expected you to harm them. Eventually, you'd give up trying to prove that you're worthy of trust.

To begin to live the truly successful life that you deserve, keep these six truths in mind:

SIX KEYS TO A TRULY SUCCESSFUL LIFE!

1. **Believe that there is a purpose for your life.** In all of the world, you are unique. From the moment you were conceived, your DNA was unique. You were "hardwired" with the seeds of a unique package of skills, talents, abilities, and personality characteristics. Implanted in you is a

dream, what I call a Life Assignment. Your dream may have been dimmed, or even long forgotten, but the fact remains that you were perfectly matched to it, and that has never changed. You have, or have access to, everything you need to find and fulfill the Life Assignment for which you were perfectly matched.

2. **Stay peaceful.** Don't give anyone the power to make you angry, sad, or frustrated. If you do, he or she wins. If you remain calm, you win. It's that simple.

3. **Stay truthful.** Don't compromise the truth for anything. Even when telling a "little white lie" is the easiest thing to do, *don't do it.* Learn how to keep your opinions to yourself, to find something kind to say, or how to tell a difficult truth gently, if necessary, so as to minimize hurting another's feelings. But adopt a zero tolerance policy for any form of deceit.

4. **Do and say what's right.** Do this in *every* situation, regardless of whether or not you think anyone is watching. Deep down, you know what's right and wrong. One easy guideline is to ask yourself if you would feel comfortable with your family and friends knowing what you're thinking about saying or doing. If not, don't say it or do it. Every time you let hurtful words come out of your mouth or do something you know isn't the best for you or someone else, you are really hurting yourself. You are dismissing opportunities that you may not even know would have come your way if you hadn't said or done the wrong thing.

5. **Choose faith.** I've experienced way too many amazing things in my life to write them all off as being coincidence,

being lucky, knowing the right people, or being at the right place at the right time. Faith is a choice. I've lived without it and I've lived with it, and I can tell you that life is infinitely better with it. My particular choice in the "faith department" is Christianity because it is rooted in love, forgiveness, kindness, patience, gentleness, humility, and goodness.

6. **Watch your words.** Say only what you want to see happen—never complain about what has or hasn't happened. Use wisdom in your communication. There are several resources you can refer to for learning to apply wisdom to your life. One guideline for wisdom that people have used for thousands of years is found in the Book of Proverbs in the Bible. Regardless of your personal beliefs, the Book of Proverbs is filled with sound advice for success. There are 31—one for every day of the month. Don't just read it; incorporate each proverb into your life. You'll be glad you did.

Now a word to those in relationships with people who have experienced pain and who can't seem to get over it...hopefully this book has given you some substantive ways that you can help that person overcome his or her pain. But how can you know if the person in your life is having trouble moving beyond their past painful experiences? Some signs include consistent irritability, meanness; or being reclusive, irrational, or generally difficult to be around. They may be making poor choices, going full speed down what you believe to be a dangerously wrong road. People who've been hurt often hurt themselves and others—often those closest to them.

So, why help them? When you invest the time and effort to help ⌐ move beyond painful experiences, you're helping to heal ⌐e healed, that person will be better able to find and ⌐lan for his or her life, often with gratitude and loyalty who invested his or her time to help.

When you help someone get traction on their path toward happiness and away from past painful experiences, you're not just helping that one person. You're acting as the catalyst for all the good that that healed, whole person will ever do for others. You will be helping his or her spouse, children, extended family, friends, boss, co-workers, neighbors, and everyone else whom that person will ever positively influence. In other words, the work of loving a wounded person into wholeness reaps exponential rewards!

Investing time in a relationship with a person who has been traumatized "loves the wounded person into wholeness." You *can* do this; you have the power. Use it to heal the hurting people within your influence. You don't have to go far to find them—they are your co-workers, neighbors, friends, and maybe even your family members. (An invaluable resource for anyone who deals with a grouchy, irritable, or otherwise broken person is a little book called *How to Hug a Porcupine.* This helpful book can give you the tools you need to help bring the healing that only good relationships can!)

Now that you have read this book, hopefully you will see yourself and the wounded people among you differently. You'll see the wounded child within the grouchy, mean, negative, or critical person in your life. You are now in a position to find something good in those people around you and point it out to them. Sometimes, you may be the only one who can see the good. Finding and telling others about the goodness and the potential within them can be life-transforming, especially for someone who has not had the experience of being valued and loved. For these people, having someone point out something good about him or her can be like healing balm on an open wound.

This ability to pour good into others crosses all social, economic, ethnic, and religious boundaries. Anyone can do this; it doesn't matter what your "station in life" happens to be, *you* can be the one who encourages others to notice the good characteristics about them, whether the person is your boss or the homeless person on the street. The receptionist who warmly greets the president of the company can be the light of his or her day. The student who encourages the principal of the school with a smile or an encouraging word; the consumer of a product who writes a letter to the CEO of a company to express gratitude for their quality product and makes that CEO's day—you never know who desperately needs to feel valued, or how far the seed of your kindness will go.

For those within your personal influence, remember that people receive advice and correction better from people who they believe like them and genuinely care about them. Identify and point out the successful survivor characteristics in the people you interact with, and you earn the right to give advice and to bring correction where necessary. Recognize, reward, and even celebrate the characteristics pointed out in this book, and watch the positive changes begin to take place in the lives of the people around you.

If you're the survivor of trauma, remember that you are not defined by the worst things you've done or by what has happened to you. Neither are you defined by your biggest accomplishments. We are each a total, goofy, awesome package. Dare to believe that you have unfulfilled potential yet to be developed and unleashed on the world. Begin right now to see yourself as the strong, tenacious, optimistic, resilient, courageous, resourceful person with an excellent work ethic who quickly shifts from passive fear to active coping. Refuse to feel any embarrassment or shame about anything in your past. Rather, mine out the characteristics from what you've been through, and use the powerful characteristics you developed and honed in adversity as the stepping stones to a successful life. When you do this, your confidence will build; you will start to stand up a little straighter, act a little bolder.

And ultimately, you and everyone around you will begin to see you as the awesome successful survivor you are!

Suggested Reading

Resilience: Discovering a New Strength at Times of Stress by Frederic Flach, M.D., K.C.H.S.

The Resiliency Advantage: Master Change, Thrive Under Pressure, and Bounce Back from Setbacks by Dr. Al Siebert

Trauma and Transformation: Growing in the Aftermath of Suffering and *Posttraumatic Growth: Positive Changes in the Aftermath of Crisis* by Dr. Richard Tedeschi, Crystal L. Park, and Dr. Lawrence G. Calhoun

Positivity by Dr. Barbara Fredrickson

The Luck Factor by Dr. Richard Wiseman

Man's Search for Meaning by Viktor Frankl

How to Hug a Porcupine by Dr. Debbie Joffe Ellis

The Happiness Advantage by Shawn Achor

End Notes

1. Friedrich Nietzsche, *Twilight of the Idols*, 1888

2. According to www.joycemeyer.org April 2015

3. Dr. Ellen Visser, from interview with Ben Sherwood, author of *The Survivors Club*, 2009

4. http://www.richardwiseman.com/resources/The_Luck_Factor.pdf

About the Author

ABANDONED AT **6** months of age to the "care" of her mentally ill grandfather and her alcoholic and drug-addicted grandmother, Rhonda spent the first 16 years of her life as a ward of the court. Most of those years were spent living in abuse and chaos, in a filthy, dilapidated shack the size of a garage (without working plumbing). Like other successful survivors, Rhonda developed the coping mechanisms that allowed her to not only survive her abandonment, poverty, hunger, and severe abuse, but to succeed in business and in life.

Rhonda Sciortino went from a humiliating beginning to living an amazing life, and she considers it part of her Life Assignment to help others find and fulfill the good plans for their lives. Rhonda lives in Southern California with her husband, Nick, near their daughter and her family.

Additional information is available at www.rhonda.org.